United States
Department of
Agriculture

Forest Service

**Technology &
Development
Program**

7100 Engineering
2300 Recreation
June 1977
Rev. December 2003
7771-2508-MTDC

Crosscut Saw Manual

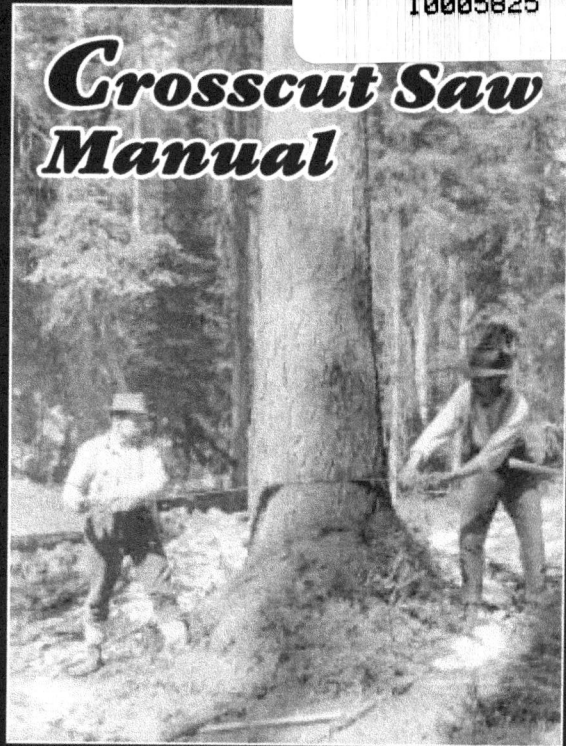

USDA Forest Service
Technology and Development Program
Missoula, MT

June 1977
Revised December 2003

Contents

Acknowledgments

This manual would never have been possible without the willing and patient teaching of Martin Winters, accomplished filer from the days when the crosscut saw reigned.

Also, special thanks to Clem Pope, friend and coworker with a mutual interest in crosscuts, and William Harlow, professor emeritus of wood technology, State University of New York, for their many helpful comments and contributions to the text.

There are persons too numerous to name here who contributed knowingly and unknowingly to this manual: sawyers, filers, and others, all of whom have something in common—knowledge about the crosscut saw and a willingness to share that knowledge. To these important individuals I give my appreciation.

Finally, my thanks to staff members of the Technology and Development Center at Missoula for their suggestions during the preparation of this manual.

—Cover photo: Northern Region Forest Service file photo by K.D. Swan, 1924, on the Flathead National Forest near Radnor, MT.

Introduction

Many readers undoubtedly have run crosscut saws in the past, and a lot of you know the difference between a good running saw and a poorly filed one. A poorly filed saw deserves the name I have often heard attributed to it… "misery whip." A well-filed saw, however, is efficient and can be satisfying to use. Only in recent years was a chain saw developed that could beat a topnotch bucker in a contest. There is a record of a 32-inch Douglas-fir log cut in 1 minute $26\frac{2}{5}$ seconds by one bucker.

Saw filers of any quality are becoming very difficult—if not impossible—to find. This manual was written so those of you who use crosscut saws can maintain them yourselves and overcome some of the misery of that ol' whip.

The manual provides a basic description of how and why a crosscut saw works, tips on building a saw vise, and some experience-tested methods as a guide for achieving a well-running saw.

Only saws having raker teeth are discussed, because they are by far the most common saws found today. This includes lance, perforated-lance, and champion tooth patterns.

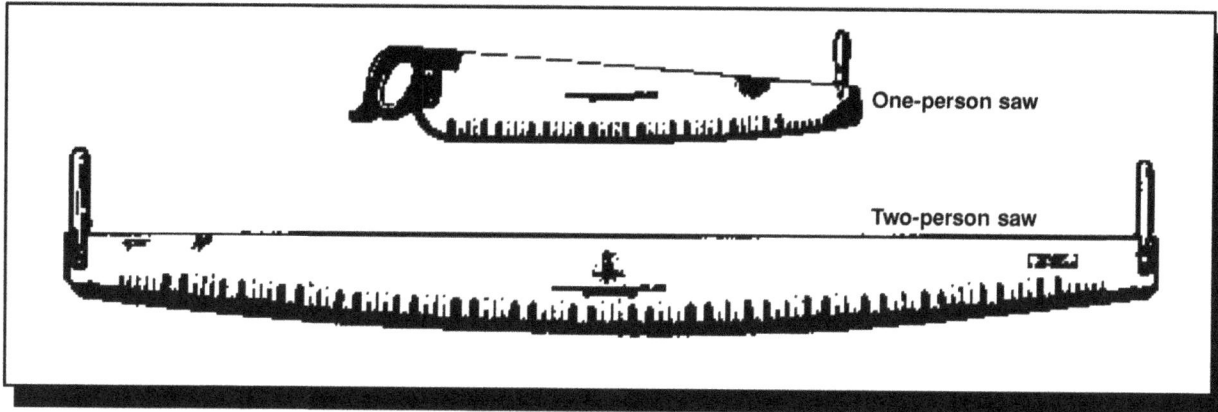

One-person saw

Two-person saw

The **felling saw** has a concave back and is relatively light and flexible. It is light so less effort is needed to move it back and forth when felling a tree. It is flexible to conform to the arc a sawyer's arms take when sawing, and it is narrow tooth-to-back, enabling the sawyer to place a wedge in the cut behind the saw sooner than with a wide saw.

The **bucking saw** has a straight back. It is much thicker tooth-to-back than the felling saw, so it is heavier and stiffer. A bucking saw traditionally is used by one person, so it is a fairly stiff saw designed to help prevent buckling on the push stroke. The more weight put on a saw, the faster it will cut, so the weight of a bucking saw is an asset.

The points of the teeth of nearly all crosscut saws lie on the arc of a circle. This result is a saw that cuts easier and faster than a straight saw. A circular contour is much simpler to maintain than a contour of any other shape (except straight).

There are three ways that the sides of a saw are finished (ground) when manufactured. Each finish affects the thickness of the saw in a particular way. These finishes are: flat, straight taper, and crescent taper.

A flat-ground saw has the same thickness everywhere. A taper-ground saw is thicker at the teeth than at the top edge of the

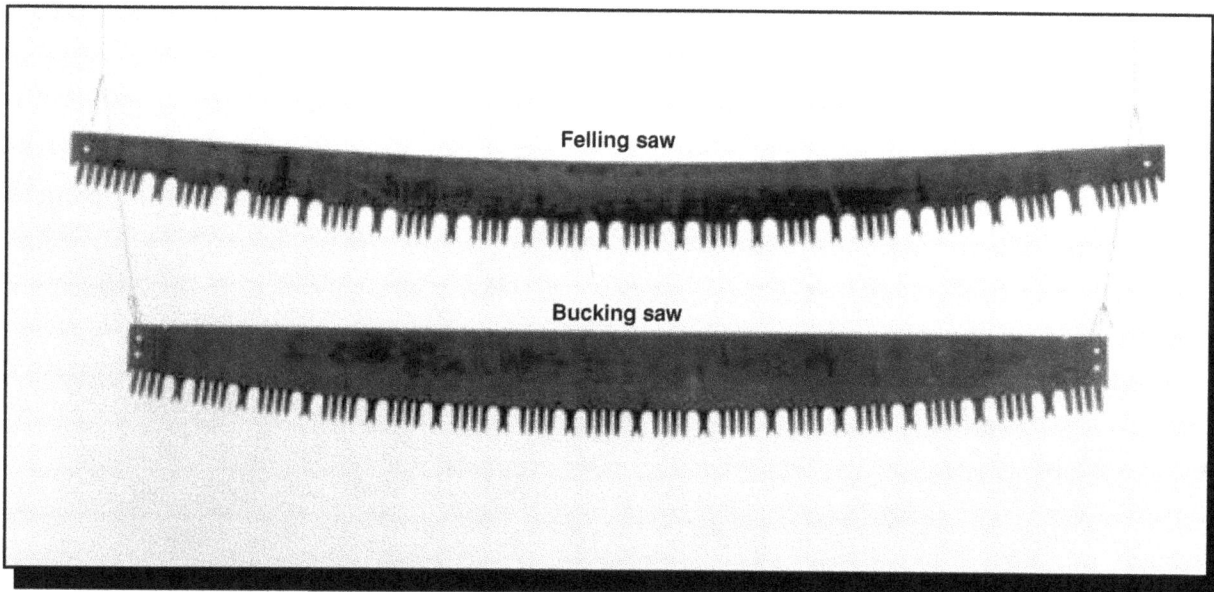

Felling saw

Bucking saw

*H*ow a Saw Cuts

The cutting teeth of a crosscut saw sever the fibers on each side of the kerf. The raker teeth, cutting like a plane bit, peel the cut fibers and collect them in the sawdust gullets between the cutting teeth and the raker teeth and carry them out of the cut. A properly sharpened crosscut saw cuts deep and makes thick shavings. On large timber, where the amount of shavings accumulated per stroke is considerable, a large gullet is necessary to carry out the shavings to prevent the saw from binding.

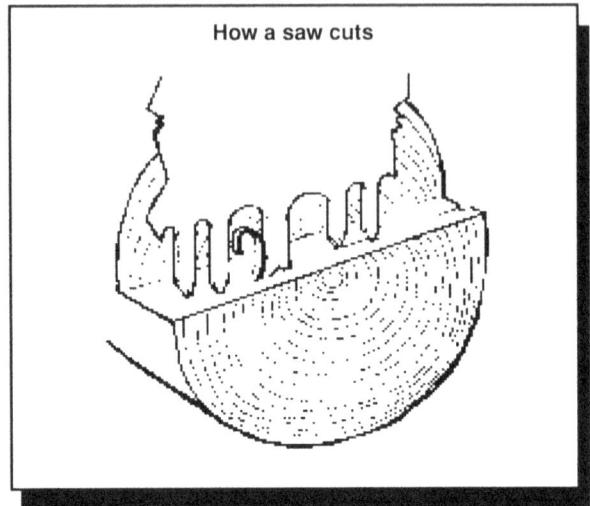

How a saw cuts

*S*aw Vise

When possible, a saw should be filed in a saw vise. A vise helps a filer do a good job.

The essential qualities of a vise are a flat surface against which a saw can be held rigidly in such a position that the teeth can be conveniently worked on.

A carpenter's handsaw vise can be used if only a few saws are sharpened, but a vise especially built for crosscut saws is best.

One way of making a vise is to use a straight, clear board, 3 by 8 inches or 3 by 10 inches, which has one edge shaped to fit the curve of a saw (**1**). If you can't obtain these sizes, two 2- by 8-inch or 2- by 10-inch boards can be glued and bolted (or screwed) together. Ensure that the surface remains flat. You can use a single 2- by 8-inch or 2- by 10-inch board, but I don't recommend this because of the lack of rigidity. The saw is held against the board with hardwood strips about $1\frac{1}{2}$ inches wide, $\frac{1}{4}$ to $\frac{3}{8}$ inch thick, and 6 to 8 inches long. Fasten the strips to the board at positions coinciding with every other raker tooth. Fasten each strip with bolts or screws. The ends of the strips should not project beyond the curved edge of the board. On each bolt or screw, place a washer as thick as the saw blade between the strip and board so the strips tighten snugly against the saw blade and hold the saw firmly against the board.

The saw should fit the vise so that the teeth project above the curved edge of the board far enough so they can be filed without the file touching the vise.

Another method of making a vise is to use two shaped 2 by 8s or 2 by 10s and clamp the saw between them (**2**). Several bolts and wingnuts through the bottom part of the vise can be used to clamp the saw between the two boards.

Mount the vise so it will rotate around its long axis. This allows the filer to change the saw from the vertical where most of the operations are done, to an oblique angle where the cutter teeth are filed or "pointed up."

To mount the vise in this way, insert a piece of threaded rod (about $\frac{5}{8}$ inch) into each end of the vise and glue or pin it securely, leaving 4 to 6 inches sticking out. Position the vise so the threaded rods are between the uprights of the bench brackets that hold the vise a couple of inches above elbow height—or a comfortable height for the filer. Wingnuts tightened on the rod ends hold the vise securely.

The vise also can be mounted directly to a workbench with hinges (**3**) so it can be tilted back for the pointing-up operation. Several stops behind the vise hold it firmly at the desired angle.

Saw vise styles

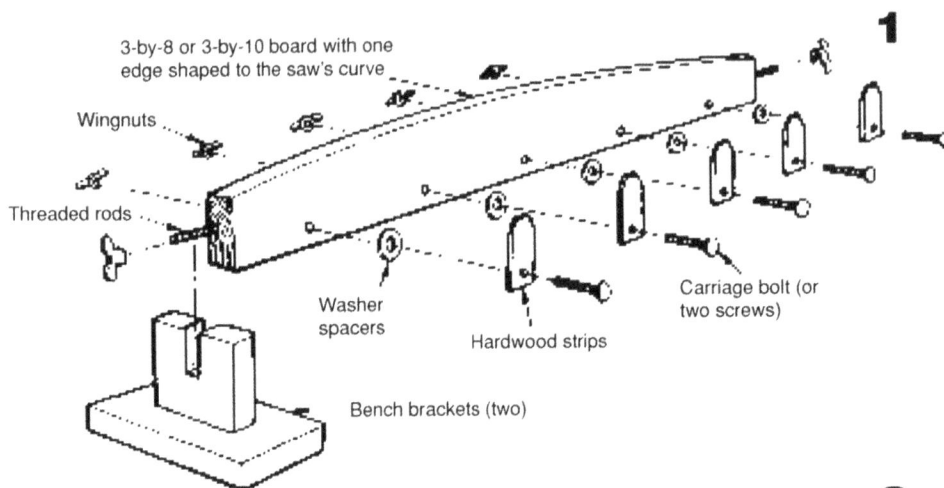

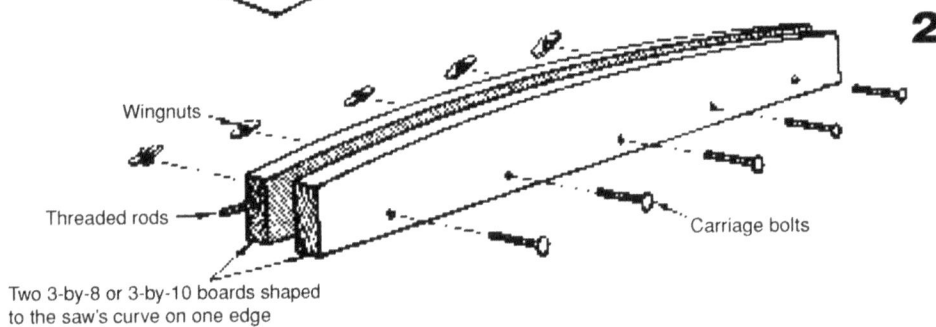

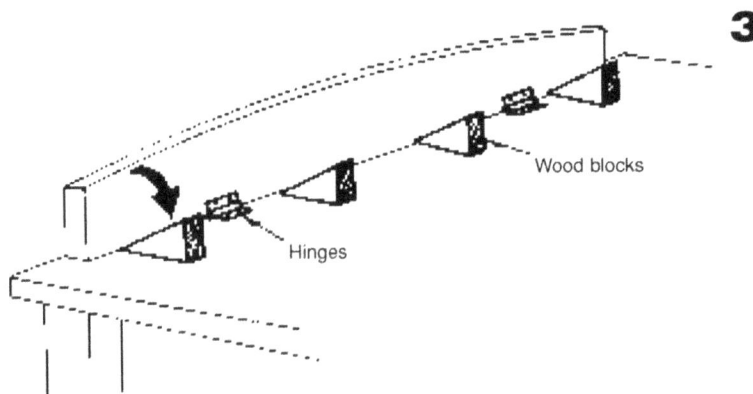

1

3-by-8 or 3-by-10 board with one
edge shaped to the saw's curve

Wingnuts

Threaded rods

Washer
spacers

Hardwood strips

Carriage bolt (or
two screws)

Bench brackets (two)

2

Wingnuts

Threaded rods

Carriage bolts

Two 3-by-8 or 3-by-10 boards shaped
to the saw's curve on one edge

3

Wood blocks

Hinges

Filing the Saw

Opinions vary among saw filers on the order of steps followed in filing a saw. Guidelines offered by saw companies differ significantly. After examining the reasons for the different orders, I prefer the following order:

- **Cleaning**—removing rust or pitch.

- **Hammering**—straightening a saw if it has bumps, kinks, or twists.

- **Jointing**—the means by which the tips of all the cutter teeth on the saw are made to conform to the circle of the saw.

- **Raker fitting**—includes shaping the raker gullet and swaging and sharpening the raker.

- **Pointing up cutter teeth**—sharpening the teeth by filing.

- **Setting**—bending the tips of the cutter teeth away from the plane of the saw, causing the kerf to be wider than the saw.

Tools necessary for:

- **Hammering**
  —Two steel straightedges about 10 to 14 inches long.
  —3- to 4-pound cross-pein saw hammer (some manufacturers call them cross-face hammers).
  —Fairly flat anvil.

- **Jointing**
  —Jointer (short or long).
  —7- or 8-inch special crosscut file (mill bastard blunt file).
  —Saw vise.

- **Raker fitting**
  —7- or 8-inch slim-taper (triangular) file.
  —Pin gauge, raker gauge, or 8- to 16-ounce tinner's riveting hammer for swaging.
  —6-inch, slim-taper file with "safe" corners (corners ground smooth).
  —6-inch mill-bastard file.
  —Saw vise.

- **Pointing up cutter teeth**
  —7- or 8-inch special crosscut file (mill bastard blunt file) for lance-tooth saws.
  —6- or 8-inch Great American crosscut file for champion-tooth saws.
  —Saw vise.

- **Setting**
  —8-ounce set hammer (or tinner's riveting hammer).
  —Setting stake or set tool, or anvil and spider.
  —Saw vise.

Cleaning

Often a filer must clean a rusty or pitchy saw. One good method is to lay the saw on a flat surface and clean it with an ax stone or a pumice grill stone. Liberally douse the saw with a citrus-based solvent to dissolve the pitch and keep the stone from plugging up with debris. Small kinks show up as bright areas when they are high spots and dark areas when they are low spots. Use only enough pressure on the cutter teeth to clean them. If metal is taken off the tips, both set and tooth length will be affected.

Hammering or Straightening

Few saws are completely straight. Although slight kinks or bumps will not cause much trouble, a straight saw requires minimum set and is less likely to buckle during the push stroke when one person is sawing...and it will cut straighter.

The saw to be straightened is hung vertically from one of the handle holes.

Hold the straightedges lightly, one on each side of the saw, so they are directly opposite each other. By moving the straightedges back and forth, as well as along the saw, any kinks or bumps can be found. If you move the straightedges with a slight twisting motion, quite small kinks can be found by the difference in resistance to twisting the straightedges. A straightedge contacting the convex side of a kink will twist more easily than one on the concave side.

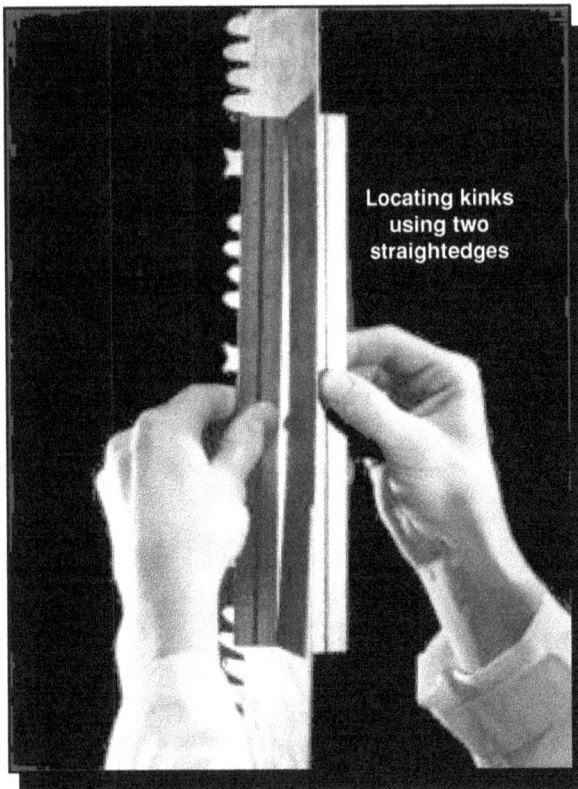

Locating kinks using two straightedges

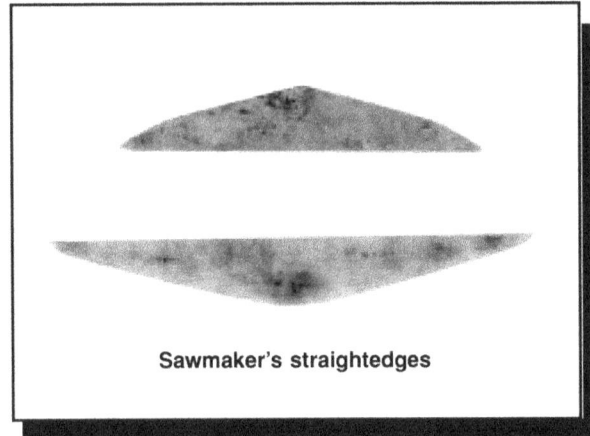

Sawmaker's straightedges

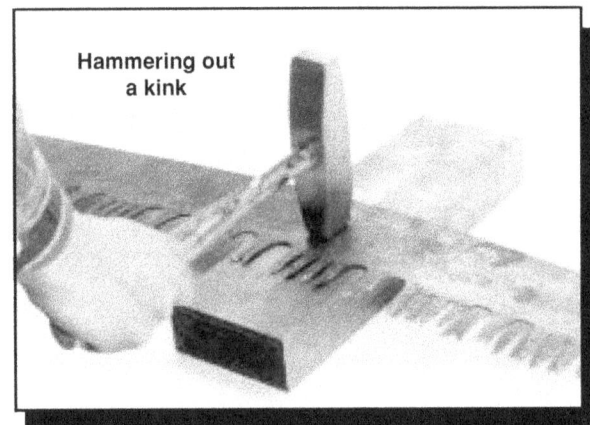

Hammering out a kink

When a kink is located, determine its shape and axis by moving the straightedges over its surface. Mark its shape with chalk or grease pencil (a wetted finger works well, too). Put the concave side down flat on the anvil, and with the appropriate face of your cross-pein hammer, strike the saw several times over the kink. (The appropriate face is the one that is fairly parallel to the kink axis). Check the kink with the straightedges and determine further action. Take care to strike the saw with the face of the hammer and not the edge. When hammering is done properly, the hammer should leave no visible mark. A slightly round-faced, 3-pound hammer can be used but results aren't as good as with a cross-pein hammer.

If it is not possible to acquire a straightedge specifically for saw work, there are acceptable substitutes. A desirable straightedge will be light, stiff, and reasonably straight. A thickness from 0.050 to 0.100 inch is acceptable, but the thinner straightedge is better. Substitutes might be a draftsman's or machinist's straightedge, or the rule on a combination square.

Jointing

The number and variety of jointers are considerable, but the principle is the same for all. They hold a file in such a way that the jointer can be run over the saw teeth to ensure the teeth all lie on the circle of the saw. There are short and long jointers. The short jointer, generally part of a combination saw tool, is by far the more common.

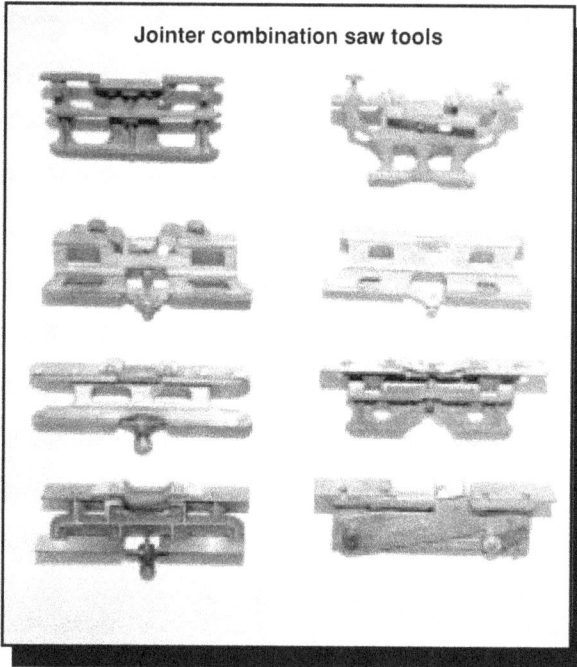

Jointer combination saw tools

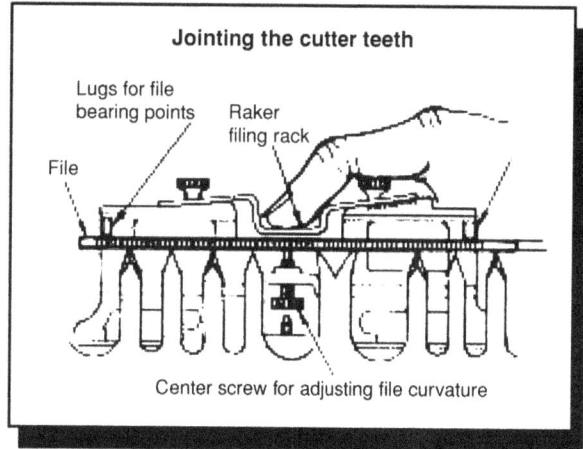

Jointing the cutter teeth

Lugs for file bearing points

Raker filing rack

File

Center screw for adjusting file curvature

Short Jointer

To use the short jointer, insert the file so it rests flat on the file supports (lugs) and adjust the screw so the file bends to conform to the circle of the saw. Make sure the surface of the file is square with the guide rails on the body of the jointer. The file may be warped or improperly seated on the supports. Insert the file so it runs in the normal filing direction. (If a file is used backward, its life will be severely shortened.) Because a new file often will cut faster than desired, a wornout 7- or 8-inch special crosscut file with the tang broken off works well.

Place the jointer on one end of the saw. Holding the jointer so the file rests on the cutter teeth, run the jointer the length of the saw using uniform downward pressure. This is important if the circle of the saw is to be maintained. It is also important to hold the guide rails on the body of the jointer in contact with the side of the saw at all times to ensure that the file is square to the saw.

After the jointer has been run the length of the saw, look at the teeth. If each tip has a shiny spot where the file has just touched it, jointing is complete. If some teeth are so short they weren't touched, repeat the process until all teeth show the mark of the file. If a tooth has been chipped or broken so it is much shorter than the rest, don't worry about it. No sense jointing the life out of a saw to make it perfect.

Long Jointer

If a long jointer is available, it achieves superior results and guarantees a round saw when used properly. A saw that has deviations from its arc (bumps or troughs) won't saw smoothly.

The long jointer operates on the principle that three points in a plane uniquely define a circle (or arc), or that there is only one circle that will simultaneously pass through three given points in a plane.

The long jointer has two "shoes" about 12 inches apart with a file mounted between them. The file can be moved up and down relative to the two shoes. Whether the shoes or the file moves is immaterial. The two shoes and the file constitute the three points that define a circle. Only two long jointers were ever commercially manufactured. One, a Gibbs jointer, was marketed by Simonds Saw and Steel Co., and the other by E. C. Atkins and Co. The shoes on the Gibbs jointer move and the file on the Atkins moves.

As with the short jointer, it is a good idea to make sure the file is square with the guide rails on the body of the jointer. This can be checked with a small square.

With the saw in a stable position, preferably in a saw vise, place the jointer about in the center of the saw. Adjust the jointer so that both shoes and the file contact the saw and tighten the adjusting nuts. By moving the jointer along the saw and observing whether the jointer rocks on the file or has space between the file and the teeth, the high and low places can be observed easily. When the high and low spots are found, adjust the jointer so the file clears all but the higher spots. This is done by placing the jointer on a high spot and adjusting it so the file and shoes will contact the saw.

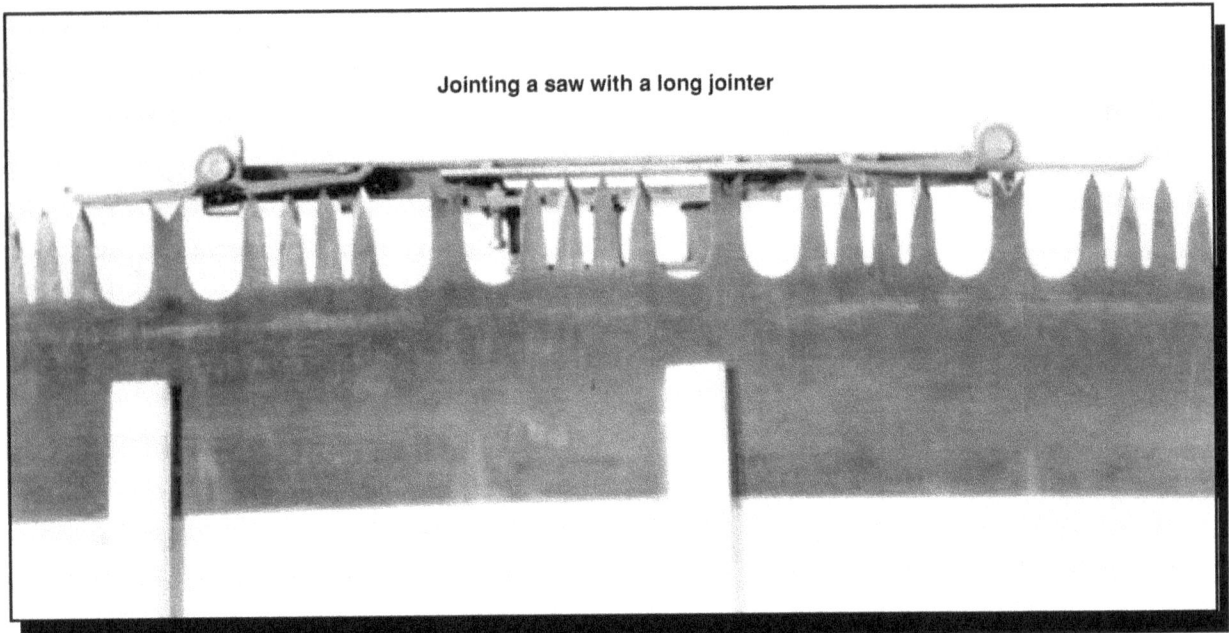

Jointing a saw with a long jointer

These are important steps. If the initial jointer adjustment were made with the file over a relatively low spot and the saw jointed with that setting, it would be impossible to get the saw into round without taking excess material off the center teeth.

With the jointer adjusted on the saw, pass it lightly and evenly from one end of the saw to the other. The very end teeth should be jointed in this process. This means dropping one shoe or the other off the end of the saw to run the file over the end teeth. The file will cut the tips off the high teeth. If—as is often the case with really worn saws—the file will not make contact toward the end of the saw, the end teeth are too long. This can be corrected by jointing the ends more severely than the center of the saw. If the teeth are particularly long, a lot of time can be saved by cutting these teeth down with a hand-held file, checking your progress periodically with the jointer.

As with the short jointer, the saw should only be jointed until all the teeth have been marked by the file (except extremely short or broken teeth). The less metal taken off the teeth, the less work the filer must do later in pointing up the teeth, and the longer the saw will last.

The end teeth of a solid-ended saw cannot be effectively jointed with a long jointer unless the solid section is filed to or below the circle of the saw.

It is possible to cut the solid end off a saw and repunch the holes for the handles.

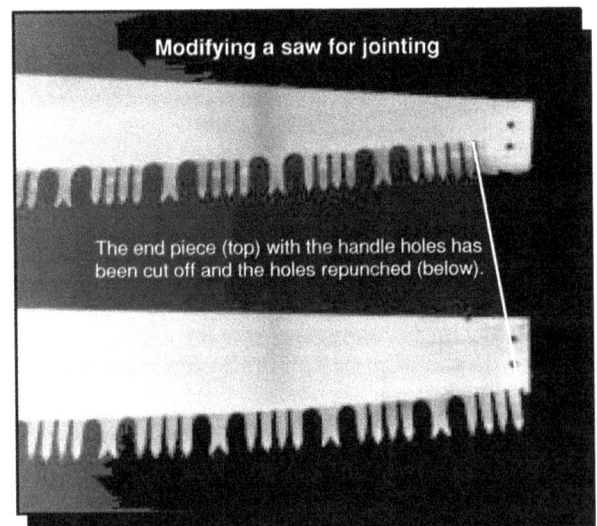

Modifying a saw for jointing

The end piece (top) with the handle holes has been cut off and the holes repunched (below).

Raker Fitting

The raker teeth remove shavings that the cutter teeth have severed from the wood. For a saw to operate efficiently, the raker must remove all the wood severed by the cutter teeth, but no more. If too little wood is removed (too short a raker), energy will be wasted because of unnecessary friction between the cutter teeth and unremoved wood. If too much wood is removed (rakers too long), it is necessary for the raker to break the uncut fibers along the edge of the chip, resulting in wasted energy and a "whiskered" shaving.

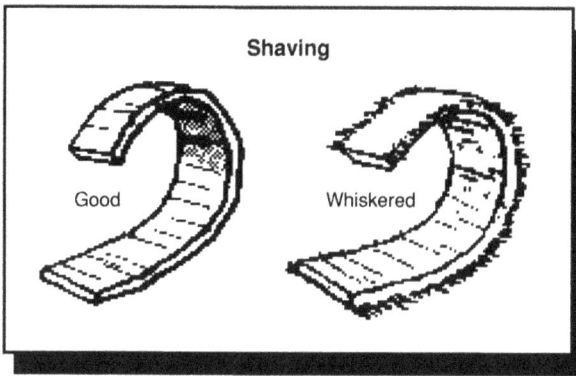

Shaving

Good

Whiskered

Because the cutting teeth exert pressure on the wood as they cut, a certain thickness of wood is compressed and springs back after the teeth pass over. As a result, fibers are not severed quite as deeply as the teeth penetrate. Consequently, the rakers following the cutter teeth must be shorter by the amount that the wood springs back, so no unsevered wood is removed. The amount of springback varies with wood type, moisture content, saw weight, and cutter tooth shape. Optimum raker depth depends on all these factors.

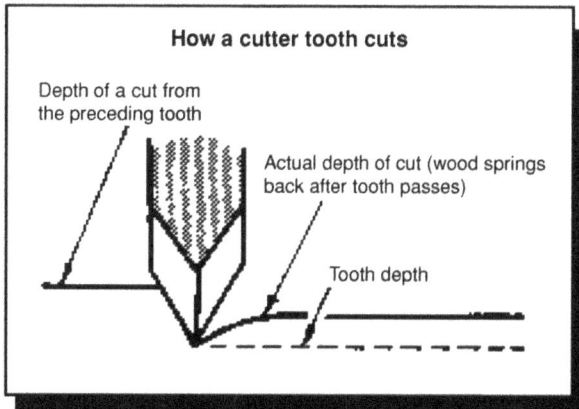

How a cutter tooth cuts

Depth of a cut from the preceding tooth

Actual depth of cut (wood springs back after tooth passes)

Tooth depth

Optimum depth is obtained by experiment, but figures vary from 0.008 inch for hard or dry wood to 0.030 inch for soft, springy wood; 0.012 inch is a good average figure to begin with.

The depth of the rakers below the cutter teeth is determined by using a tool called a raker gauge or raker depth gauge.

The raker depth gauge is generally part of a combination saw filing tool of which numerous varieties were manufactured. The essential feature of all of them is a hardened steel filing plate with a slot cut in it a little wider than the thickness of a saw and a little longer than the distance between the two tips on a raker. This is held on a frame so that when the gauge is placed over the raker, the top of the filing plate is the same level as the desired raker depth. The raker tips are cut to the level of the plate with a file. The height of the filing plate is adjustable.

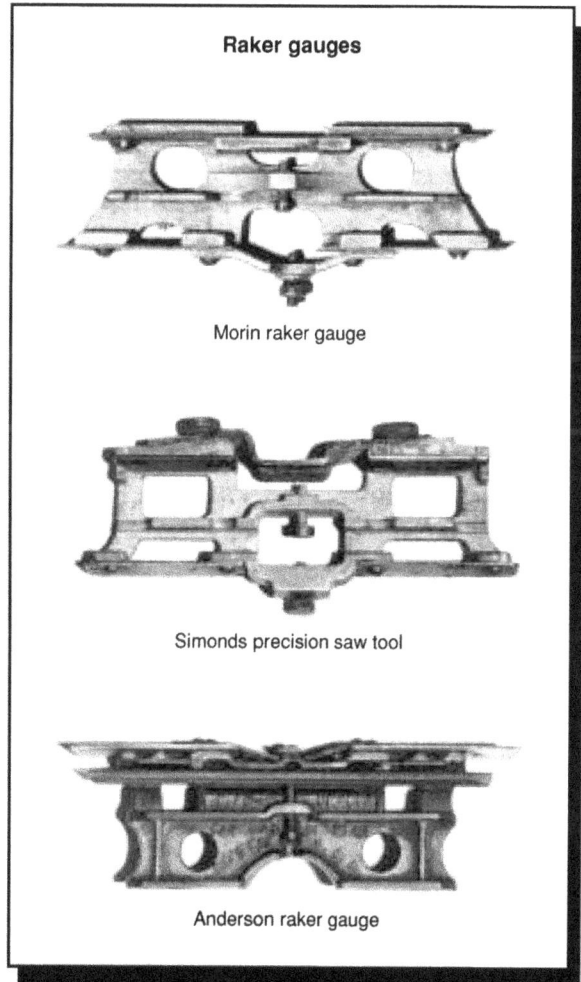

Raker gauges

Morin raker gauge

Simonds precision saw tool

Anderson raker gauge

Adjustment of the depth gauge is straightforward. With the simpler gauges, such as the common Morin gauge, two screws hold the filing plate to the frame, and the adjustment is made by putting pieces of paper between the frame and the filing plate. The Simonds precision saw tool adjusts by sliding the filing plate up and down two ramps. A scale on the side of one of the ramps indicates the depth of the top of the filing plate. Each division of the scale corresponds to 0.004-inch difference in the height of the filing plate. A notch opposite the scale on the filing plate indicates the desired raker depth. The Anderson gauge adjusts by moving the plate up and down with a screw. Only minor adjustments should be made using the screw, because large deviations could break the brittle filing plate. Paper between the filing plate and the tool frame can be used for large adjustments. The Anderson gauge is the only known gauge with a sloped filing plate. Instead of filing the raker tip flat, it establishes a 15-degree clearance angle.

"slow" running saw. The swaged raker is considerably more difficult to shape, but the results are a superior running saw. The reason for the difference is apparent when one remembers that the raker acts like a chisel to remove the shaving. Much less energy is required to remove wood from a board if a chisel is held at a low angle to the board than if it is held vertically. Swaging results in a raker tip that is similar to a chisel held at a low angle to the wood.

Fitting Straight Rakers

The teeth of a saw are formed by punching, so the gullets of most saws are rough. With a 7- or 8-inch, slim-taper file, dress (smooth) the outside face of the rakers from the raker tip to the bottom of the sawdust gullet. Make sure the file is held square with the saw. This will provide clean, sound metal for

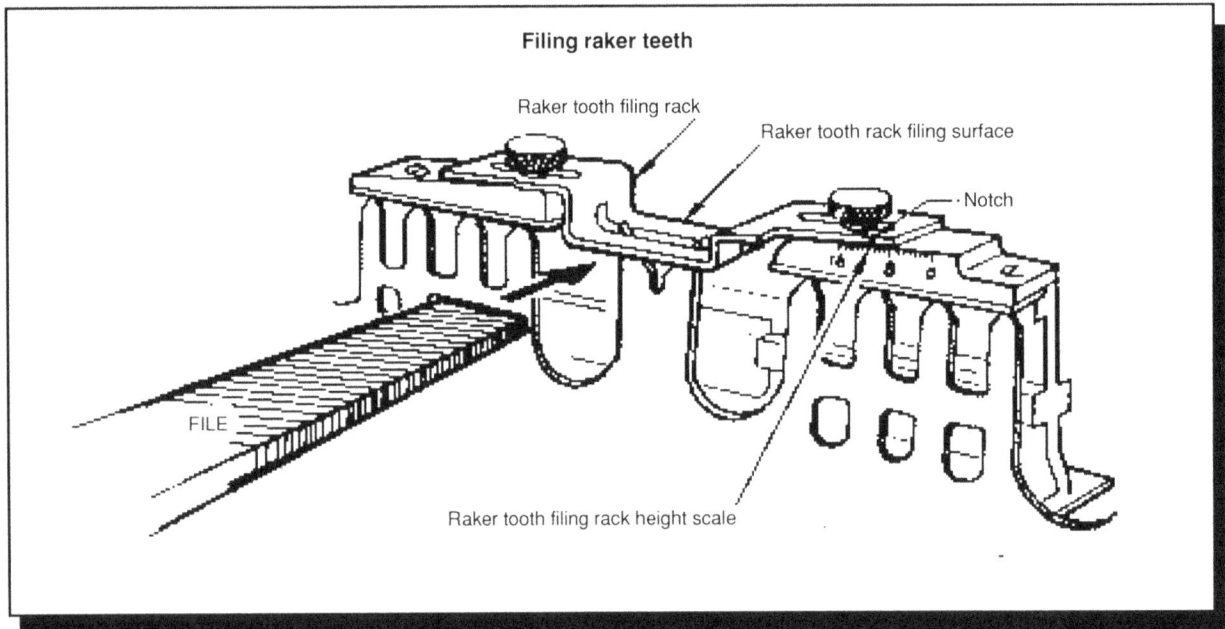

Filing raker teeth

Raker tooth filing rack

Raker tooth rack filing surface

·Notch

FILE

Raker tooth filing rack height scale

One way of checking the setting of a raker gauge is to file a raker using the gauge. Place a straightedge between the two cutter teeth on each side of the filed raker and measure the relative height with a feeler gauge placed between the raker and straightedge.

There are two basic ways a raker can be shaped before it is filed to its proper depth using the raker depth gauge. These are known as straight (plain) and swaged rakers. There are advantages and disadvantages to each method. The straight raker is by far the easier to file, but it results in a relatively

the cutting edge of the raker, cause less friction between the outside face and the shaving, and aid shaving removal.

Next, file the raker to the proper depth. Place the properly adjusted raker gauge on the saw so the raker fits in the slot in the filing plate. Hold the gauge so it rests firmly against the tops of the cutter teeth as well as the side of the saw. Run a file across the raker tips until they are even with the top of the filing plate. Once the raker tips have been filed, the rakers must be sharpened. With a 7- or 8-inch slim-taper file, shape the raker gullet to the approximate shape (shown next), rounding

Shaping a raker tooth (straight raker)

Flat spot

Round gullet

About a
60° angle

Tools needed to fit swaged rakers

Combination saw-filing tool and pin gauge

Swaging hammers

"Safe" corners

Six-inch, slim-taper file. Equip with a knuckle
guard and handle.

Six-inch, mill-bastard file. Equip with a knuckle
guard and handle.

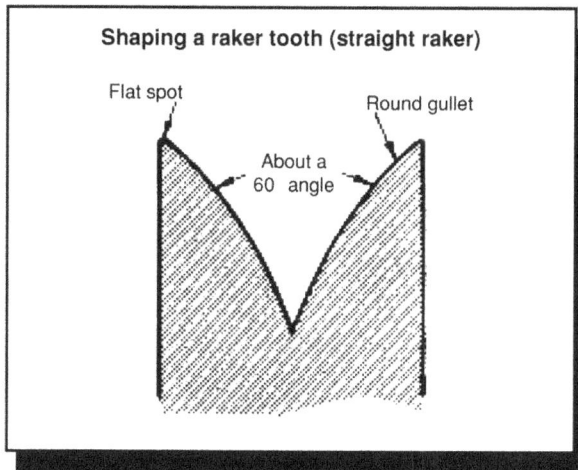

the gullet out to the tip until the flat spot on the top *almost* disappears. If the tip is overfiled, it changes the raker depth. If not filed enough, the flat spot acts like a "sled runner" and does not allow the edge to work properly.

If you're using an Anderson-type gauge, this step is not critical. The clearance angle has been established and a good-sized "flat" spot can be left. Make sure the end of the filing slot in the Anderson gauge is held firmly against the tip of the raker. Otherwise, the raker tip will be filed too low.

Fitting Swaged Rakers

Swaging is forming the leading edge of the raker into a curve so it more efficiently picks up the shaving. It is done by striking a prepared raker tip on the inside face with a hammer to bend the tip outward in a smooth curve.

Tools necessary are a pin gauge, 8- to 16-ounce hammer for swaging (16-ounce hammer preferred), raker gauge, 6-inch, slim-taper file with "safe" corners, and a 6-inch, mill-bastard file. A pin gauge generally is part of a combination saw-filing tool.

I know of no hammers specifically designed for swaging. A swaging hammer should have a face small enough to allow you to strike the raker tip with the center of the hammer face. The best substitute for a swaging hammer appears to be a tinner's riveting hammer. A swaging hammer should weigh about 16 ounces. A lighter (8-ounce) hammer can be used, but a 1-pound hammer is easier to use.

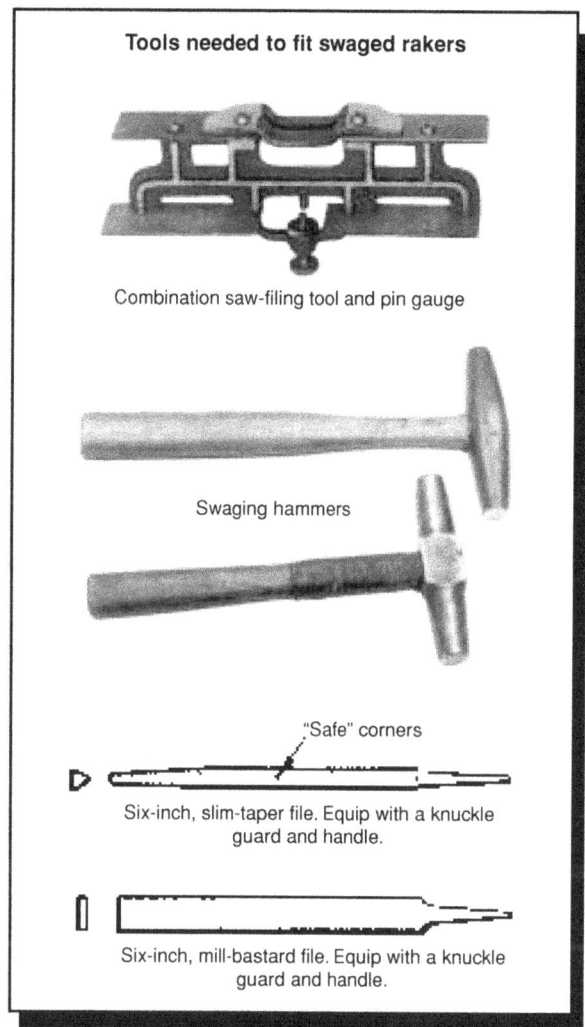

To Prepare the Raker—File it approximately to the shape shown at right with the slim-taper file. The exact shape depends on whether the raker is straight or if it has been swaged before. The objective is to shape the tip so it can be bent without breaking but retain enough thickness to prevent bending during use. The cutting angle should be between 30 and 40 degrees.

The raker is now ready to be "swaged to the pin." This means bending the raker by striking the inside face of the raker tip with a hammer until the tip just clears a preset screw (called a pin) on a combination saw tool.

Preparing a raker

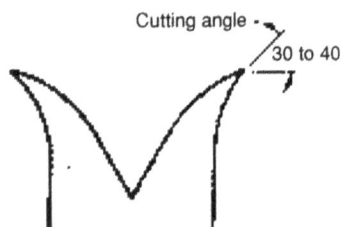

Cutting angle

30 to 40

This is also a good shape for a finished raker.

Gauging rakers with the pin gauge on the combination saw tool

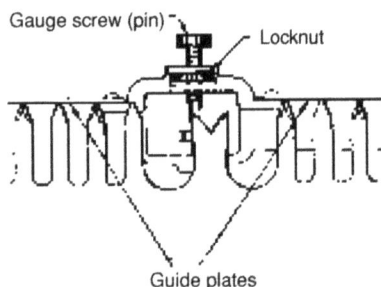

Gauge screw (pin)

Locknut

Guide plates

Striking the inside face of the raker tip with a hammer

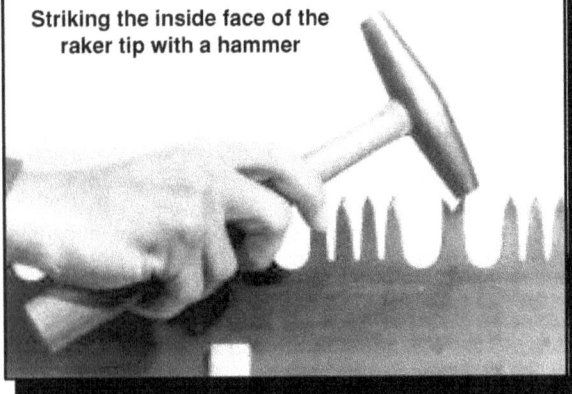

The pin is adjusted so the swaged raker is 0.002 to 0.003 inch higher than the finished raker depth. This is done by first filing a raker to depth using the raker gauge (which has already been set using methods described previously). Next, place the pin gauge over the raker and adjust the pin (screw) depth so a 0.002- or 0.003-inch feeler gauge will just pass between the raker tip and the pin. Check the clearance again after tightening the locknut.

To Swage a Raker—Strike the raker tip a square blow and check the height with the pin gauge. If it is still too high, continue alternately swaging and checking until the raker tooth just clears the pin. Keep an eye on the shape of the bend. The outside face of the raker should bend in a smooth arc. A kinked raker tip will be difficult to swage next time the saw is filed, and it will quite possibly break. If the tip begins to kink, the hammer probably is being used too high on the tip. If it won't bend, the tip may be too thick or the hammer is being used too low on the tip. Often in the case of a new saw or a used saw with straight rakers, it will be necessary to partially swage the tip. Thin the tip with the file and continue swaging.

There is no pat answer to the question: "At what angle is the raker struck?" This will vary with the shape of the raker tip and must be learned from experience. Keep an eye on the desired swage shape. Knowing where to strike the tip will come with experience.

Some saws are so hard and consequently brittle that there is a possibility of breaking raker tips when swaging. If a saw is so hard that a fairly new file keeps slipping while the filer is shaping the raker gullets, or if a raker actually breaks when being swaged, the rakers should be tempered.

To temper the raker, polish one side of each raker until it is shiny. Place the saw in a vise. Heat the top three-fourths of the tooth uniformly using a propane torch. As it gets hotter, the color will go from light straw to brown, to deep purple, to dark blue, to light blue, to a light yellow color. Opinions differ on how far to temper the rakers (or to heat them to what color). A compromise seems to be between light blue and the second yellow. A suggestion would be to first temper to light blue and if trouble is still experienced, temper again to the second light yellow. Don't heat into the body of the saw because it may cause the saw to warp. Be very careful about playing the torch flame on the raker tips—they heat very fast, making them extremely easy to overheat. The result is a soft raker that will bend in hardwood and will not hold an edge.

Once the rakers are "swaged to the pin," the tips are dressed on the outside face. To dress the swaged tip, a 6-inch, slim-

15

taper file with safe corners is passed lightly across the under edge of the swage to square it up and establish the rake angle. It is most important not to nick the raker with the edge of a file. A nick can cause the tip to break off during swaging or while the saw is being used. This is the reason for the ground safe corners on the dressing file. After dressing the outside face and rake angle, joint exactly as with the straight-style raker. As with straight rakers, a trial depth of 0.012 inch is good for average conditions.

The last step is to dress the sides of the rakers. The swaging process often widens the raker at the tip. This can be corrected by holding a 6-inch mill-bastard file flat against the raker and saw and making one or two light vertical strokes.

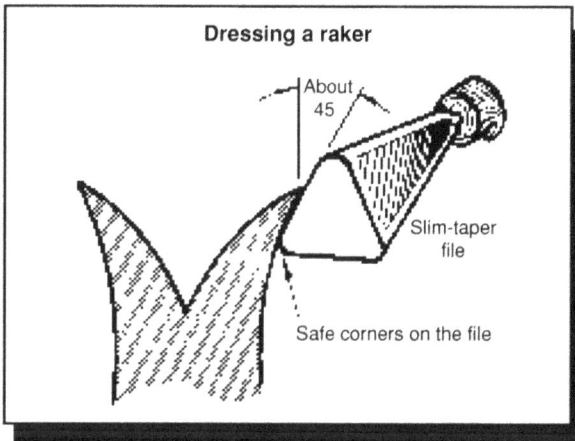

Dressing a raker

About 45

Slim-taper file

Safe corners on the file

Repairing Bent Rakers and Cutter Teeth

To check for bent rakers, make up a spider (set gauge) for zero clearance on an unbent raker. A bent raker can be found easily by using the spider in the same manner as for checking cutter tooth set (see *Setting*).

To straighten a bent raker, the concave side of the raker is placed on an anvil and hammered until the tooth is straight. Badly bent cutter teeth could be straightened the same way.

Broken Raker Tip

A broken raker tip allows the other tip on the raker to bite too deeply on the cutting stroke, causing the saw to catch just as it does with a long raker. File the unbroken tip shorter, about 0.005 inch initially. If it still catches, continue filing.

Pointing Up Cutter Teeth

To point up the cutter teeth, tilt the vise away from you at about a 45-degree angle. With the vise tilted, the flat spot on each tooth caused by jointing should appear bright. To accomplish this, place the main light source in front so you can see a good reflection from the flat spot. A wide set of windows (preferably without direct sunlight) works well. Two 4-foot fluorescent lights mounted end to end on a wall supply uniform lighting regardless of weather conditions. Avoid point sources of light such as incandescent bulbs and direct sunlight.

For filing the teeth, a 7- or 8-inch special crosscut file is used. The tooth shape illustrated below is good for general purposes.

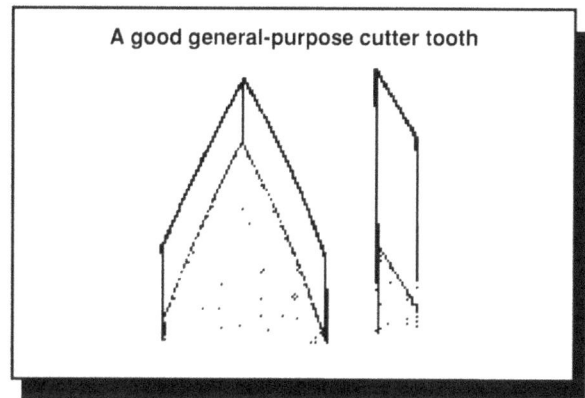

A good general-purpose cutter tooth

The stroke should be more nearly up and down than across the tooth. The main point to keep in mind when filing a cutter tooth is to file just enough to almost make the flat spot from the jointing operation disappear. Overfiling upsets the relationship between the cutters and the rakers and also results in a weak point. A slight rolling or rocking motion of the file generates a

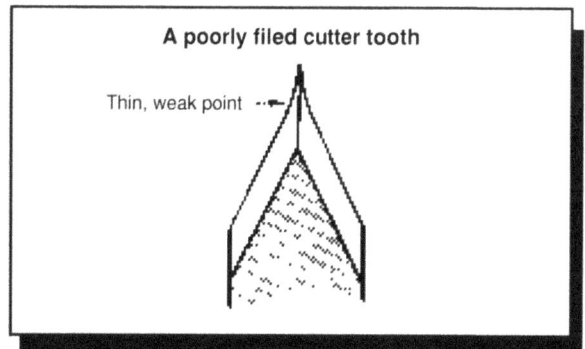

A poorly filed cutter tooth

Thin, weak point

slightly convex filed surface and results in a more durable tooth. Because of the set, a tooth whose filed surface is flat will develop a concave cutting edge and a thin, weak point.

The more pointed a tooth is filed, the deeper it will sink into the wood and the "hungrier" a saw will be. However, a sharply pointed tooth will wear faster than one less sharply pointed. The consensus is that there should be less bevel on a cutter tooth for hardwood than for softwood.

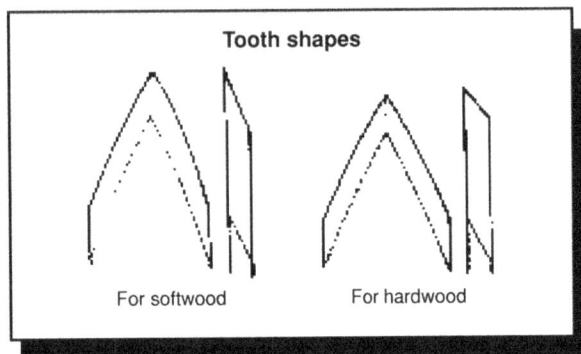

Tooth shapes

For softwood   For hardwood

As the tooth is being filed, it is a good idea to periodically remove the burr that forms on the back side of the tooth, because the burr can obscure the true tooth shape. Remove the burr with a whetstone or a *light* stroke of the file across the tooth back— *just enough to remove the burr*. The back side of the tooth must not be filed, because it may cause the saw to bind. The burr also can be removed with a piece of hardwood.

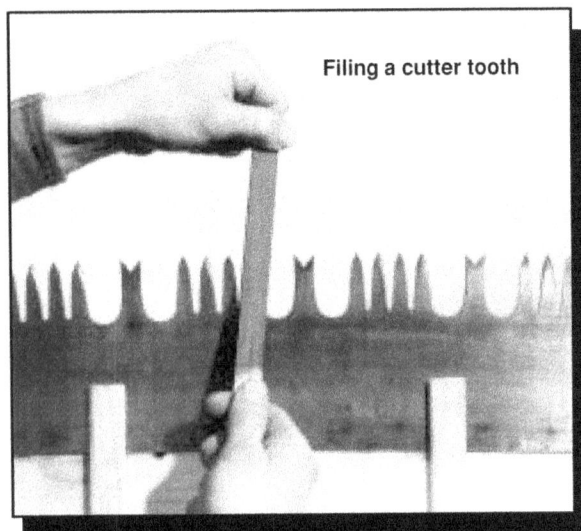

Filing a cutter tooth

After all the teeth are filed, hold a fine stone flat against the saw. Pass it over the teeth to remove any residual burrs, especially at the tips of the teeth. A burr under the spider would cause an error in the tooth set.

Setting

To set a saw is to bend the tip of each cutter tooth a slight amount away from the plane of the saw. Just as alternate teeth are sharpened opposite each other, they are set opposite to each other. Setting helps prevent binding by cutting a kerf that is slightly wider than the saw. The amount of set required depends on the type of saw used and the type of wood being cut. A saw should be set only as much as required to keep it from binding. More set than necessary results in more work to make a wider kerf and a saw that flops in the cut with the possibility of a curving cut. The set required can vary from almost nothing for a crescent-taper-ground saw in dry hardwood to 0.030 inch for the same saw in soft, punky wood. A set of 0.010 inch is a good preliminary figure. Flat-ground saws require more set.

There are two basic methods of setting: spring setting and hammer setting. Spring setting is done by using a tool with a slot that fits over the top of the cutter tooth. The tip of the tooth is bent the required amount. This method is not recommended because of the possibility of bending the whole tooth and the fact that a tooth doesn't seem to hold a spring set well.

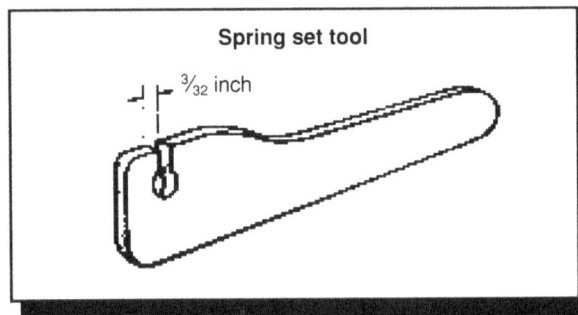

Spring set tool

$^3/_{32}$ inch

There are several ways of hammer setting a saw, only one of which is recommended. Two other methods are briefly discussed for familiarity.

One method uses a setting stake. The setting stake is placed on a log or block and the wedge fully driven in to keep the stake in a firm position. The blade of the saw is laid on the stake with the point of the cutter tooth projecting over the bevel about $\frac{1}{4}$ inch. The tooth is then struck with the set hammer as shown.

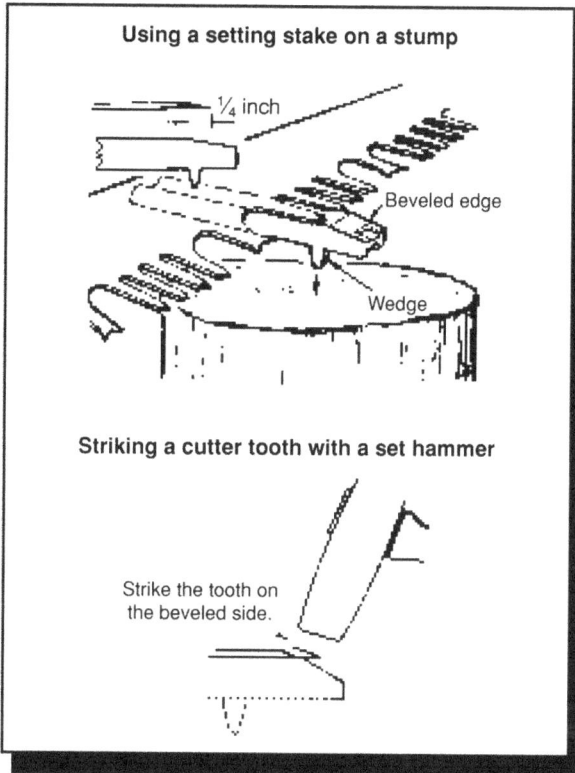

Using a setting stake on a stump

$\frac{1}{4}$ inch

Beveled edge

Wedge

Striking a cutter tooth with a set hammer

Strike the tooth on the beveled side.

Another method uses a tool that is placed over the cutter tooth and is struck with a hammer.

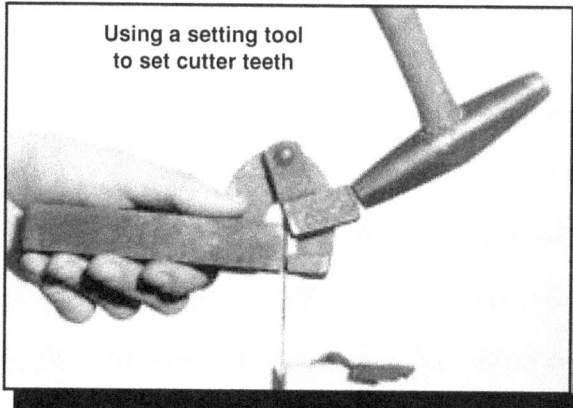

Using a setting tool to set cutter teeth

A third method uses a hand-held anvil and a hammer.

The principle is the same for the three methods: the tooth is bent over an anvil with a direct or indirect hammer blow.

The first two methods have definite disadvantages over the third. They each require a specialized tool, and they are slow. To check the set in the first method, the saw must be lifted off the setting stake.

The second method is a little more efficient because the saw doesn't have to be moved. The tool can be used with the saw in a vise. There is no chance of a misdirected hammer blow marring the tooth. However, there's a good chance of banging and dulling the tooth tip with the tool, and the tool isn't really designed for removing set if too much is put into the tooth.

The third method is recommended because of its speed and accuracy. Necessary tools are an 8-ounce set hammer, a set anvil, and a spider (set gauge).

There doesn't appear to be a current manufacturer for a hammer specifically designed for setting. A setting hammer should have a fairly small face. A large face such as most ball-pein hammers have is difficult to use for setting without hitting adjacent teeth. The best substitute for a setting hammer is a tinner's riveting hammer that weighs about 8 ounces.

Anvils were manufactured in a variety of sizes and shapes. Most were made of hardened steel and had a bevel to bend the tooth over. There is no known manufacturer for hand-held anvils. Any piece of steel that can be held comfortably in the hand, has a flat face, and weighs about 2 pounds will work. A piece of $1\frac{1}{2}$-inch-diameter shaft about 5 inches long works well. It is not necessary to have a bevel—simply set the tooth over the edge of the face.

The spider (set gauge) is used to measure the tooth set. To measure the set for which the spider is adjusted, place it on a flat surface so that the feet on the three short legs contact the surface. With light pressure on the three short legs, measure

Spiders

the clearance under the fourth foot (or longer leg) with a feeler gauge. A piece of plate glass or a mirror will work for the flat surface, though it is wise to check the spider several places on the surface so errors caused by irregularities can be averaged.

As indicated earlier, a set of about 0.010 inch would probably be satisfactory for an average cut using a felling saw. About 0.015 inch of set is required for a heavy bucking saw.

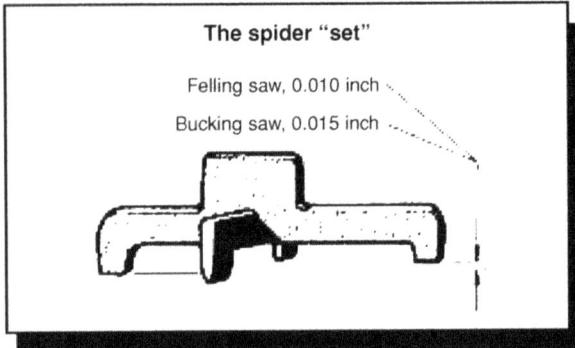

The spider "set"

Felling saw, 0.010 inch

Bucking saw, 0.015 inch

To adjust the spider for less set, place it on a flat carborundum stone, and while putting pressure on the short crosspiece, grind the feet down until it measures correctly. For more set, shorten either end of the long crosspiece. It is important that the foot at the end of the long leg is flat and parallel to the plane defined by the other three feet. This assures a constant reading no matter where the tip of the cutter tooth contacts the foot. This can be checked by lightly grinding that foot while the two feet on the short crosspiece are in contact with the stone and observing the resulting pattern on the foot.

To set the saw, place an anvil on the point side of the tooth and strike the tooth on the beveled side with a set hammer. The bevel on the anvil should be about $\frac{1}{4}$ inch below the tip of the tooth and the direction and placement of the hammer blow such that the tip of the cutter tooth is bent over the bevel. Be sure to strike the tooth squarely. If the tooth is struck a glancing blow with the edge of the hammer face, the point of impact will be badly marred. This sometimes work-hardens the metal enough that a file won't cut it and it may make the tooth more susceptible to breaking.

It is also important to keep the face of the anvil parallel to the plane of the saw during setting. If it is held at an angle, the tooth will be twisted after it has been set. Check the set with the spider. If the vertical legs rock, there is insufficient set and the procedure should be repeated. If the horizontal legs rock, there is too much set and some must be taken out. Move the anvil nearly to the top of the cutter tooth and strike a light blow.

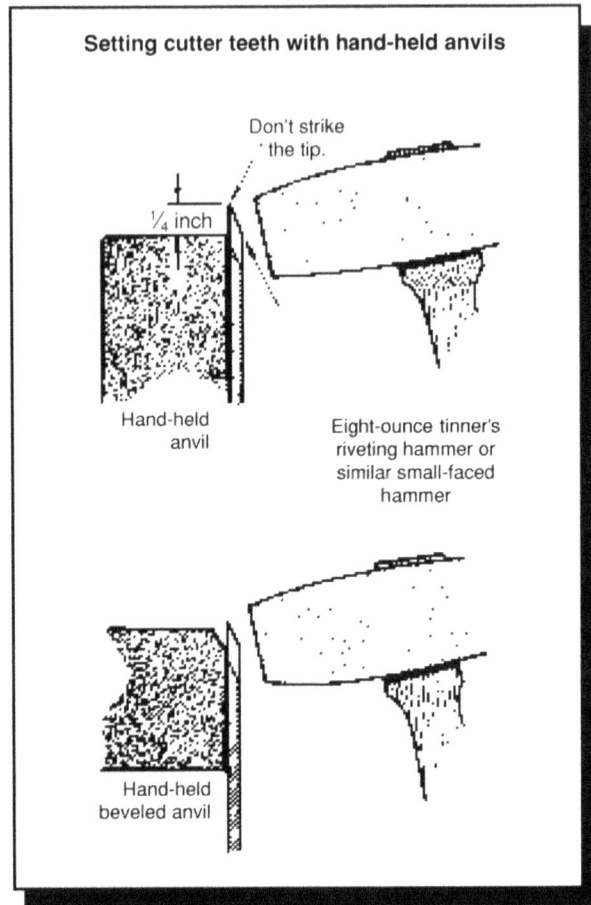

Setting cutter teeth with hand-held anvils

Don't strike the tip.

$\frac{1}{4}$ inch

Hand-held anvil

Eight-ounce tinner's riveting hammer or similar small-faced hammer

Hand-held beveled anvil

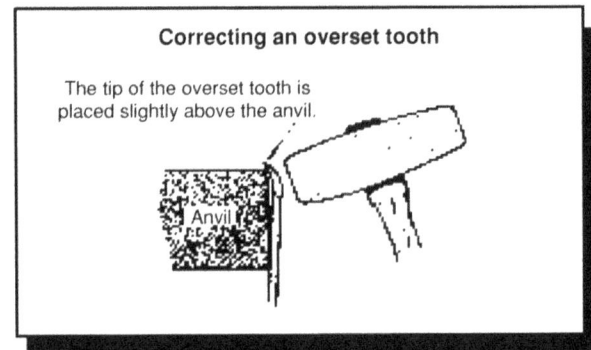

Correcting an overset tooth

The tip of the overset tooth is placed slightly above the anvil.

Anvil

Sometimes a tooth will be bent from a point below the filed part of the tooth. This can be determined by checking with the spider up and down the tooth. If this is the case, place the anvil on the tooth just below the bend and straighten it by hammering the opposite side of the tooth just above the anvil.

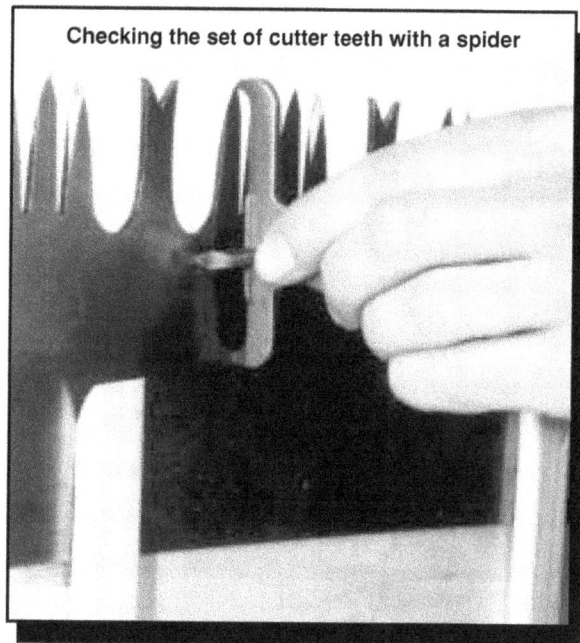

Setting cutter teeth

Checking the set of cutter teeth with a spider

Testing a Saw

Make a cut in an average log. A properly running saw cuts without jumping or catching, doesn't bind, makes a straight cut, and makes thick shavings without "whiskers."

Jumping or catching is most often caused by a raker out of adjustment. Check the shavings. If a raker is too long (high), the shavings will have whiskers. The most likely cause of a high raker is overfiled cutters. To correct a high raker, lay the raker gauge lightly over the raker and file it down. Use as little pressure as possible so the points of the cutter teeth in contact with the raker gauge are dulled as little as possible.

If most shavings have whiskers on just one side, either the filing plate on the raker gauge is not square to the plane of the saw (resulting in an unsquare raker cutting edge) or the file in the jointer was not square to the plane of the saw (resulting in the cutter teeth on one side being longer than the other). The solution is either refile the saw after correcting the tool problem or use the saw as is.

If the saw cuts hard and pulls whiskered shavings, the rakers are too long (too little raker depth).

If thin, papery shavings are pulled, the rakers are likely too short. To check further, push down hard on the saw while cutting. If this does not produce thicker shavings with whiskers, the rakers are probably too short. Another test is to saw a small pole or to saw so only a few teeth contact the wood. If whiskers are not produced, the rakers are too short.

Examining shavings for sharpening problems

Thin shaving—raker teeth too short

Whiskered shaving— raker teeth too long

Another cause of a catchy or jumpy saw is uneven set.

Binding can be caused by too little set or a curving cut.

A curving cut can be caused by several things: a kinked saw, too much set allowing the saw to flop in the cut, uneven set that pulls the saw to one side, or a sawyer bending or twisting the saw as he cuts (not a fault of the saw, but a problem that might be blamed on the saw).

Choosing and Using a Saw

Felling saws have been used by trail crews instead of bucking saws for several reasons. They are light and flex easily to conform to a backpack or horse pack. Although a felling saw is generally used by two persons, when it is filed properly and the cut is close to vertical, it can be used easily by one. However, with cuts much off the vertical, the free end will droop on the push stroke and oscillate violently on the return stroke.

Saws made today have solid ends (the teeth don't run to the ends of the saw). These saws are adequate for bucking and felling. But for finishing some cuts, for example, a log lying in the dirt, you need a saw with teeth right to the ends. When acquiring a crosscut saw, choose the tooth-ended saw.

An effective saw guard can be made of a section of old firehose, preferably rubber-lined, that has been slit along its length. A guard that is removed often can be fastened with Velcro to speed removal and replacement.

To carry a saw, lay it flat across your shoulder with the teeth guarded and facing away from your neck. Remove the rear handle so it won't catch on brush or limbs. In a group, you should walk last in line.

A saw should have better protection than firehose when being transported. An accidental blow with a tool or hitting the saw against the side of a vehicle will cause the teeth to cut through the hose and be dulled. One effective way to transport a saw is between two pieces of plywood that are bolted together.

The first step in cutting a log is swamping. Remove any brush, plants, and so forth, that may interfere with the saw. Something as seemingly insignificant as a blade of grass between the teeth and kerf can jam a saw.

Check the lay of the log and decide what will happen when the log is cut. Will it roll, jump, or drop? Plan your cuts accordingly. Sometimes it will be safe only to have one person sawing, such as when the log is on a slope. Saw from the uphill side.

Before making the cut, remove the bark where the saw will pass. Bark often has dirt in it, and some say bark can dull a saw rapidly.

When cutting green wood, sap may stick to the saw blade and gradually build up to where the saw blade will bind in the kerf. To prevent this, the saw blade should be lubricated occasionally or when the blade gets sticky. Traditionally, kerosene was the solvent of choice to loosen resin stuck on the saw. Today, citrus-based solvents are recommended because they do a good job and present less risk of causing health problems or environmental contamination.

Solvents, for this purpose, traditionally were kept in a small, flat hip flask that was carried comfortably in a back pocket. If the cork in the flask had two to three small grooves cut down its length, the blade could be covered evenly with a thin film of kerosene by whisking the corked bottle along the saw blade.

Today, plastic squeeze bottles, spray bottles, and pressurized aerosol cans offer different—although not necessarily better—alternatives to corked flasks.

Make sure the saw doesn't get in dirt or rocks while finishing a cut. Make the last few strokes with the end of the saw so

An old firehose used as a saw guard

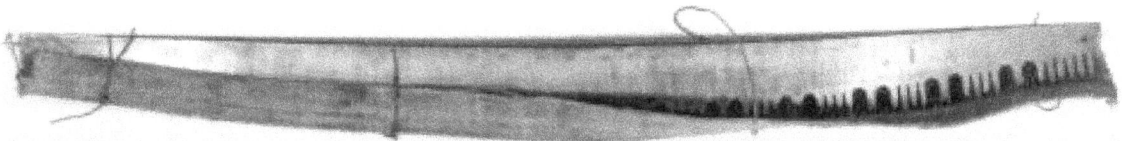

that if the saw gets in the dirt, only the end teeth are dulled. Put a piece of bark under the log, if possible, when there is a chance of running the saw into the dirt. If necessary, dig the log free where the saw will pass. The object is to keep the saw sharp as long as possible.

Though not recommended, a saw can be touched up in the field. An improvised vise can be made by cutting a slot in a stump or log and wedging the saw into the slot with some wood slivers. Usually only a file is available in the field, so only the cutter teeth can be touched up. Remember, don't overfile. It is better to leave the saw just a little dull than to shorten the tooth by overfiling.

If a saw has a raker that is catching badly, it can be shortened a slight amount until the saw cuts smoothly again. Be sure to shorten only the offending raker. It is sometimes difficult to determine which one is catching.

A leaning tree might have grown so the fibers are quite compressed on one side. It may be possible to only sink the saw teeth in only a couple of inches before the teeth bind. When this happens, chop out the severed wood with an ax, saw a few more inches and repeat the process.

Often, a log will be lying so that the kerf begins to close on the saw before a cut is completed. This occurs when the wood is under compression as when a log is supported at the ends and the cut is made in the middle. In some cases, the cut can be continued by driving a wedge into the kerf behind the saw. This won't work when there is not enough room to drive a wedge to open the kerf, so the log must be cut from the bottom, or "underbucked."

Generally, this should be done by one person with one handle removed from the saw. This reduces the chance of the saw being kinked or broken if the log carries it to the ground. To underbuck, plant an ax in the log so the handle can be used as a support for the back of the saw. Cut a small notch in the handle for a guide. Some lubricant in the notch will let the saw cut easily and reduce ax handle wear. The spring of the ax handle will hold the saw in the cut with uniform pressure. A log or rock can be placed under one side of the cut to hold up the log so it will be less likely to carry the saw to the ground as the cut is completed. A mechanical underbucker also can be used in place of an ax.

Use an ax for support to underbuck a log.

23

*H*andle Positions

How a saw cuts is determined to some extent by how the handle is put on the saw and how the handle is held. Assume the saw is making a vertical cut with the teeth pointing down. With the handle pointing up, a pull stroke will be easier the farther you hold your hands toward the end of the handle. The push stroke will be harder. On the other hand, with the handle pointing down, the opposite occurs. In saws that have two holes on each end (generally bucking saws), changing the handle position from the lower to the upper hole will have the same effect as moving your hands several inches up the saw handle.

The difference in force necessary to make a saw stroke under different handle positions is due to the different downward forces applied to the saw. For example, with the handle up, a push stroke increases the downward force on the saw causing the teeth to sink deeper into the wood. The result is a deeper cut that requires more energy. On the pull stroke, a slight upward force is applied to the saw.

Storing Saws

A saw should be stored straight. Leaving it bent (such as around a firepack) will bow the saw. A stored saw should be well lubricated. Canola oil or other environmentally friendly lubricants offer alternatives to petroleum-based oils as long as they inhibit rust.

Glossary

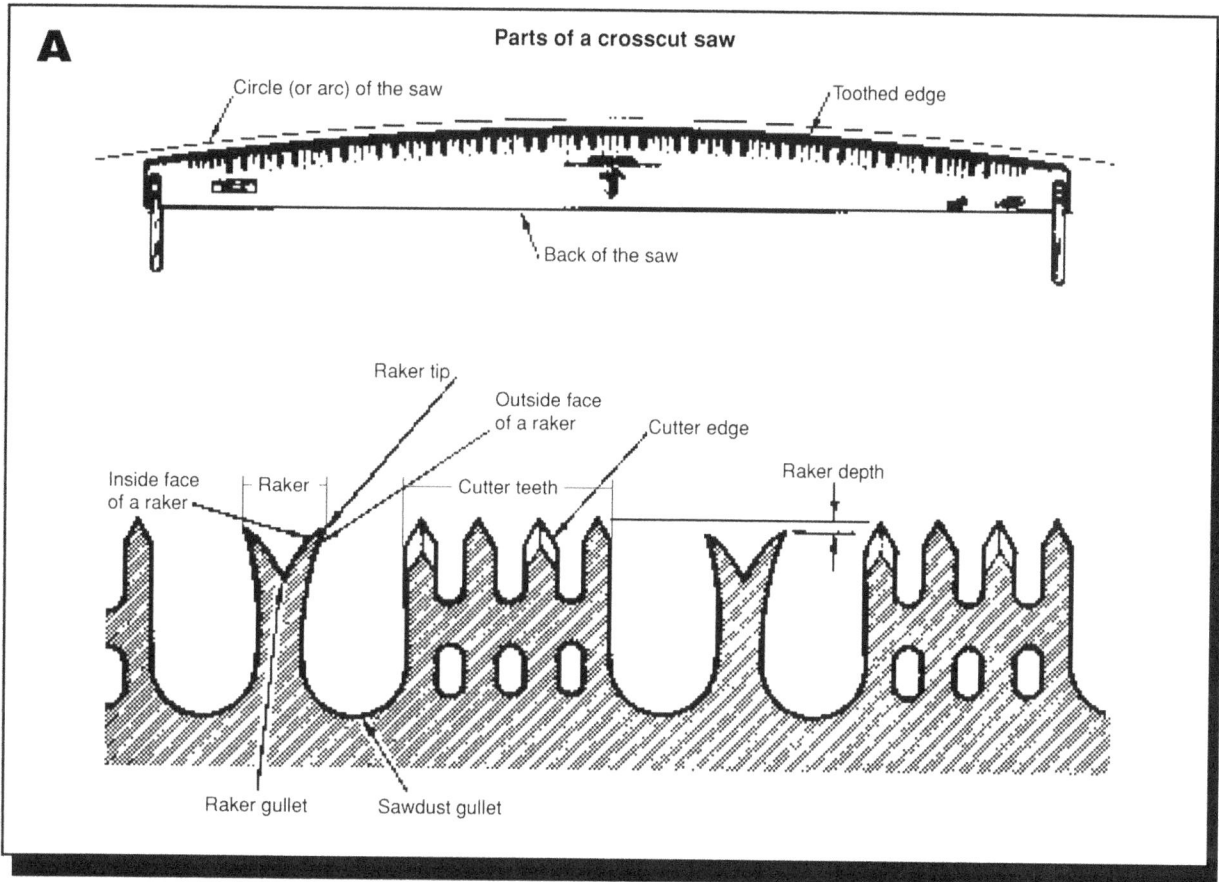

Back of the saw—(figure A) The edge opposite the toothed edge.

Bevel—(figure B) The bevel of a cutting tooth is the angle the intersection of the two filed surfaces makes with the plane perpendicular to the plane of the saw.

Circle of the saw—(figure A) The toothed edge of most crosscut saws lies on the arc of a circle.

Clearance angle—(figure C) The angle the inside face of the raker tip makes with the direction of saw travel.

Cutter tooth—(figure A) The tooth that scores the wood on each side of the kerf.

Inside face—(figure A) Face of a cutting raker tip that faces the raker gullet.

Jointer—(figure D) Tool used to file the cutter teeth so the tips all lie on the circle of the saw.

Kerf—Slot the saw makes while cutting.

Outside face—The face of a cutting raker tip that faces the sawdust gullet.

Pin gauge—(figure E) Gauge used to determine when the raker has been swaged to the desired depth.

Plane of the saw—The plane that passes through the saw equidistant from both sides of the saw.

Rake angle—(figure F) Angle that the outside face of a raker tip makes with the line perpendicular to the tangent of the saw circle.

Raker—The tooth on a crosscut that clears the shavings from a kerf.

Raker gauge—(figure G) Used to gauge the final raker depth.

26

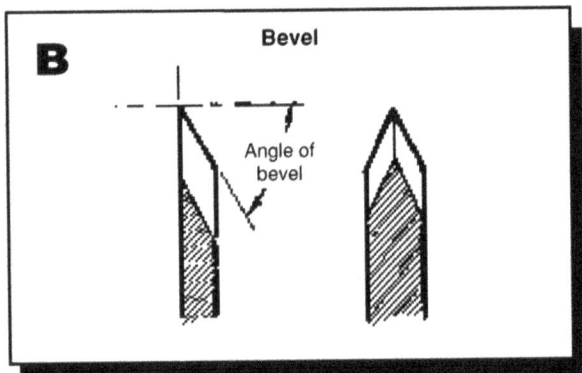

B Bevel

Angle of bevel

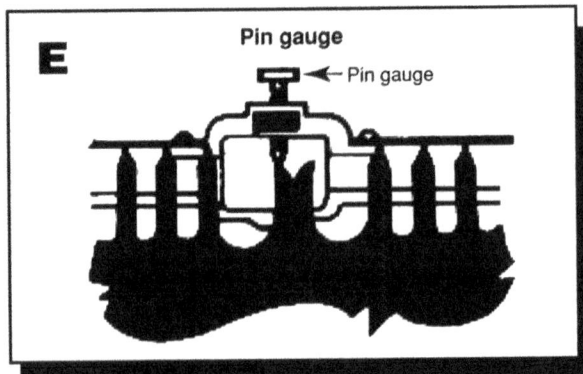

E Pin gauge

← Pin gauge

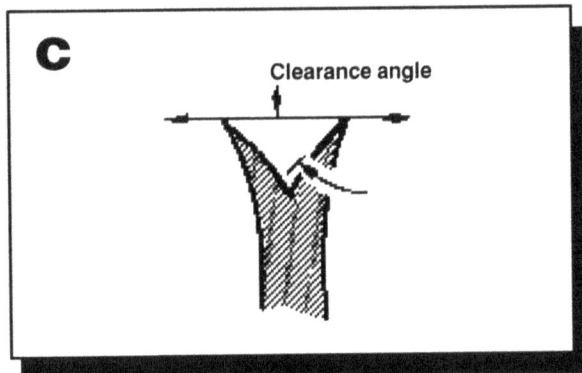

C

Clearance angle

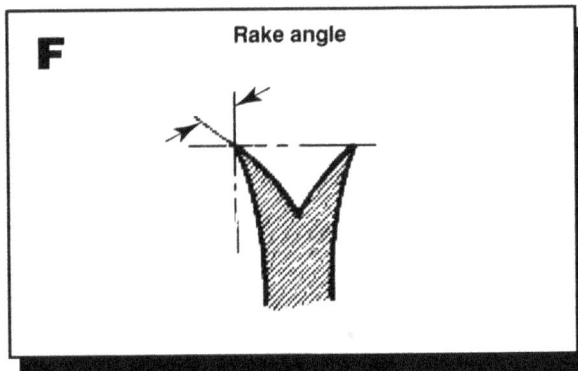

F Rake angle

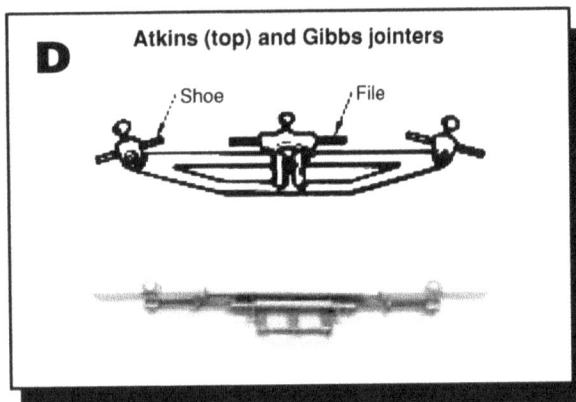

D Atkins (top) and Gibbs jointers

Shoe

File

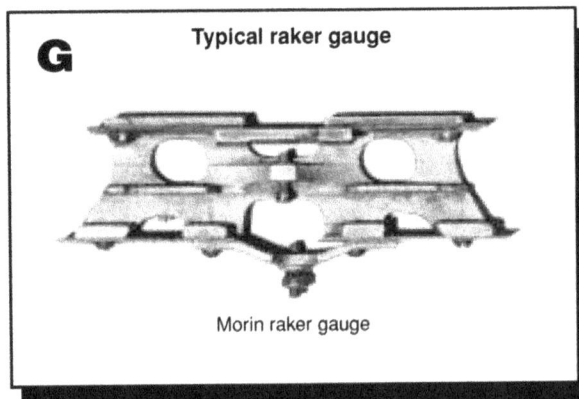

G Typical raker gauge

Morin raker gauge

Raker depth—The difference in height between raker and cutter teeth.

Raker gullet—The "V" notch in a raker tooth.

Raker face—See outside and inside face.

Raker tip—Supports the cutting edge of a raker.

Sawdust gullet—The gullet between a raker and a cutter tooth.

Set—(figure H) The distance by which the tip of a cutter tooth is bent away from the plane of the saw.

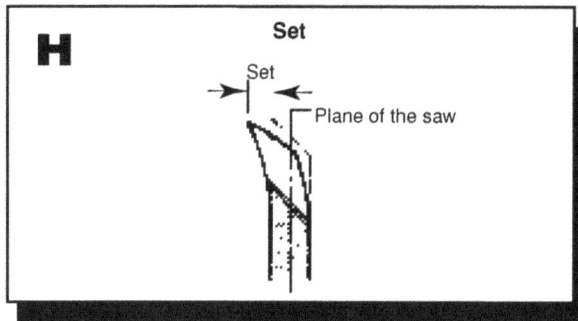

H

Set

Set
Plane of the saw

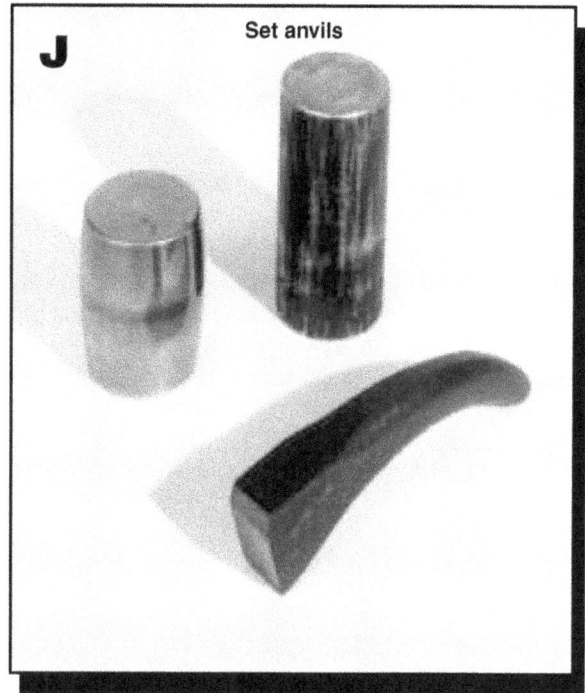

J

Set anvils

Set anvil—(figure J) A block of metal over which the tip of a cutter tooth is bent when setting.

Set stake—A tool used as an anvil for hammer setting the cutter teeth.

Spider—(figure K) A gauge used to determine when the set is correct.

Swaging—Putting a curve in the outside face of a raker tip, generally by hammering on the inside face.

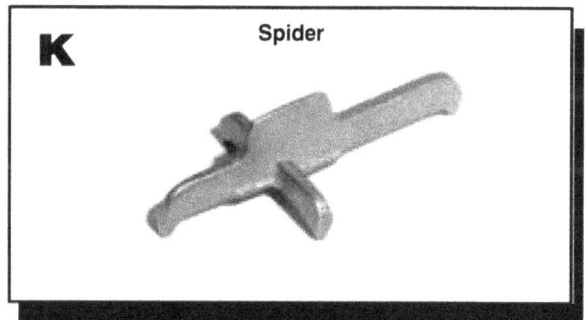

K

Spider

Notes

Notes

Single copies of this document may be ordered from:

USDA FS, Missoula Technology and Development Center
5785 Hwy. 10 West
Missoula, MT 59808–9361
Phone: 406–329–3978
Fax: 406–329–3719
E-mail: *wo_mtdc_pubs@fs.fed.us*

Electronic copies of MTDC's reports are available on the Internet at:

http://www.fs.fed.us/eng/t-d.php?link=pubs

For further technical information, contact Brian Vachowski at MTDC.

Phone: 406–329–3935
Fax: 406–329–3719
E-mail: *bvachowski@fs.fed.us*

Forest Service and Bureau of Land Management employees can search a more complete collection of MTDC's documents, videos, and CDs on their internal computer network at:

http://fsweb.mtdc.wo.fs.fed.us/search

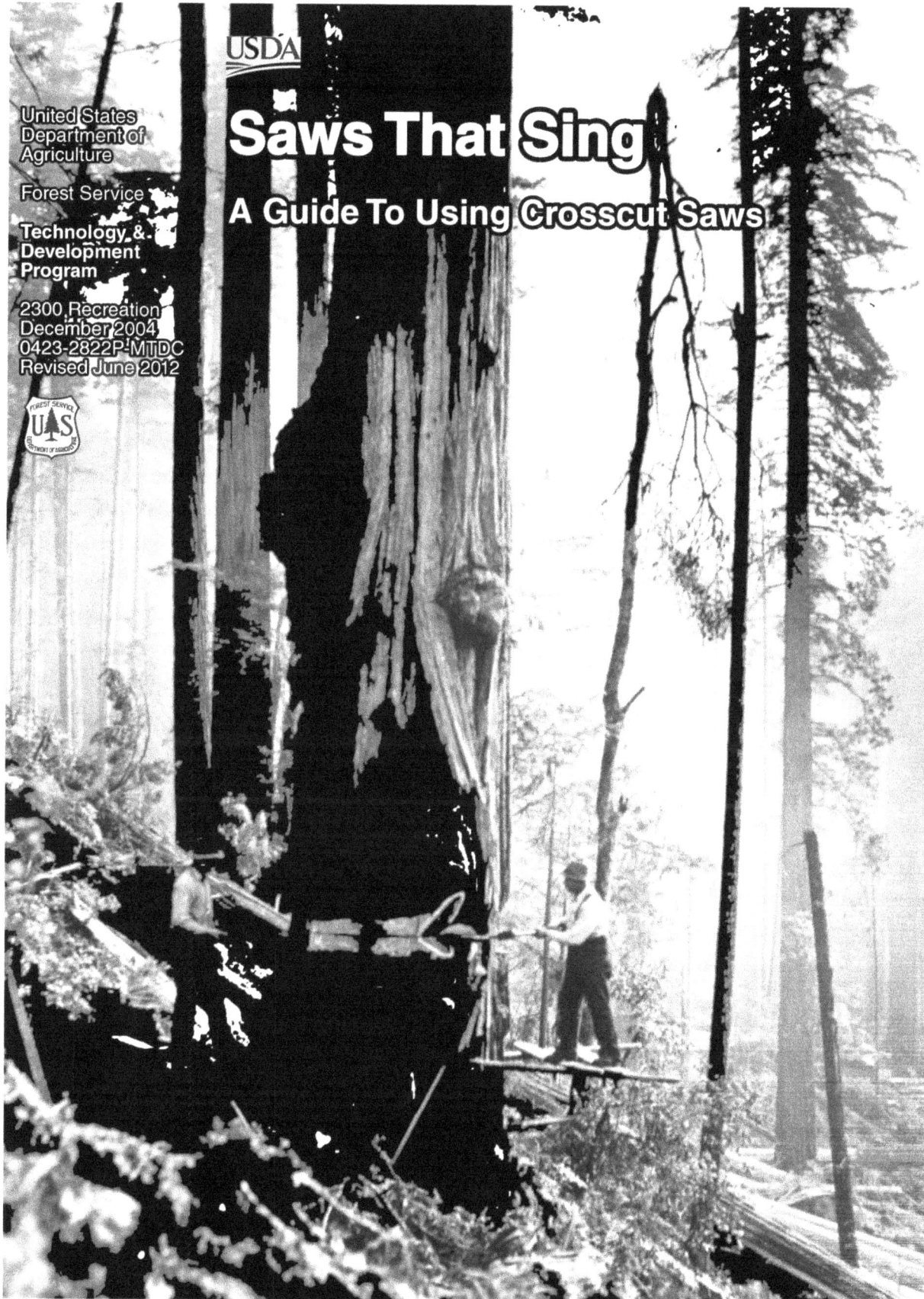

USDA

United States
Department of
Agriculture

Forest Service

**Technology &
Development
Program**

2300 Recreation
December 2004
0423-2822P-MTDC
Revised June 2012

Saws That Sing

A Guide To Using Crosscut Saws

Contents

Introduction

After working in the woods from Alaska to Arizona for more than 35 years, I've developed a profound appreciation for the precision and usefulness of the crosscut saw. There is an unfilled demand today for skilled crosscut saw users, particularly in the nearly 35 million acres of wilderness managed by the United States Department of Agriculture, Forest Service. My goal is to present tried-and-true techniques for using, appreciating, and caring for vintage crosscut saws.

I do not cover everything. Sharpening, a complex and exacting art, is left for the reader to discover in Warren Miller's excellent publication, *Crosscut Saw Manual* (1977, rev. 2003). I also will not cover complex felling techniques. I will focus on several topics:

- The saws themselves, with particular emphasis on good handles.
- The selection, function, and use of wedges. Wedges are used differently with a crosscut saw than with a chain saw.
- Bucking logs. Bucking comprises 90 percent of the trail work done with crosscut saws.

A condensed version of this text is included in the USDA Forest Service's Chain Saw and Crosscut Saw Training Course (Wolf and Whitlock 2006). Space and training time did not allow for its full inclusion there, so this book provides a more detailed reference. This 2007 revision includes updated safety information.

The USDA Forest Service requires crosscut saw users working for or on behalf of the agency to receive the required training and to be certified to perform the specific crosscut saw work they plan to do. Reading this book is not enough to provide the required training or to receive certification.

Most of what has been written about how trees and logs react to being cut with a chain saw was adapted from knowledge obtained from crosscut sawyers. Whether a tree or log is cut with a chain saw or crosscut saw, its reaction to the laws of physics will be the same. While the principles of bind and gravity are the same regardless of the tool, how you deal with them is often quite different, depending on whether you are using a chain saw or a crosscut saw. I'll go into some detail about the correct crosscut saw techniques to help you understand these differences.

Historical Origin of Crosscut Saws

The crosscut saw did not come into common use in Europe until the mid-15th century. These early saws were rectangular with handles that fitted into sockets forged into each end of the blade. Early saws had a plain tooth (also called peg tooth) design. Over the next 400 years, numerous saw patterns developed. Many countries and regions had their own "national" patterns. Saws started to appear with a curve both on the back as well as on the toothed edge. But as late as 1900 in Europe, the plain and the "M tooth" pattern were the most common.

Imported saws were used in Colonial America, and by the mid-1800s they were being manufactured in this country. However, it wasn't until about the 1880s that saws were used for felling timber. During the golden age of crosscut saws, from 1880 to 1930, numerous saw and handle styles, tooth patterns, types of steel, and methods of grinding were developed (figure 1).

Figure 1—Crosscut saws ruled the woods from 1880 through the 1930s. A lot of effort was invested to improve and perfect this versatile tool.—*USDA Forest Service photo, K.D. Swan, 1924, Flathead National Forest*

The machinery to make these vintage saws began to disappear by the 1950s, as crosscuts were replaced by power saws. Today, no taper ground crosscut saws are manufactured.

Crosscut saws manufactured today, except possibly some of the custom competition saws, generally do not have the same high quality of materials or workmanship as earlier saws. This is reason in itself to value our vintage saws.

Nostalgia may be one reason to learn how to use crosscut saws safely, but an even better reason is for management in designated wilderness, where mechanized or motorized equipment is prohibited by law. Here, traditional tools like crosscut saws and axes are needed to clear trails, cut firewood, manage wildland fires, and maintain or restore administrative buildings. In wilderness, a well-tuned crosscut saw is usually the tool of choice for felling trees and bucking logs.

Outside of wilderness, crosscut saws are the tools of choice:

- In areas of seasonal closures, such as wildlife nesting areas, because crosscut saws are quiet.
- When chain saws and internal combustion engines are prohibited because of fire restrictions.
- In situations involving miles of hiking and little cutting (minor trail clearing and smokejumping, for example) where the light weight of a crosscut saw makes it much easier to carry than a chain saw.

More and more, I see trail managers and others discovering that it's cheaper and more efficient to switch off the chain saw and pick up the crosscut. Some trail contractors have found that they pay lower worker's compensation insurance premiums when they use crosscut saws rather than chain saws.

With the right training and a sharp saw, it is amazing to see the esprit de corps and crew cohesion that develop among younger fire and trail crew members as they learn, master, and apply their crosscut saw skills.

Types of Crosscut Saws

One-Person Crosscut Saws

A one-person crosscut saw's blade is asymmetrical. The saw has a D-shaped handle. The saw also has holes for a supplemental handle at the point (tip) and the butt (near the handle). The saws are usually 3 to 4½ feet long (figure 2).

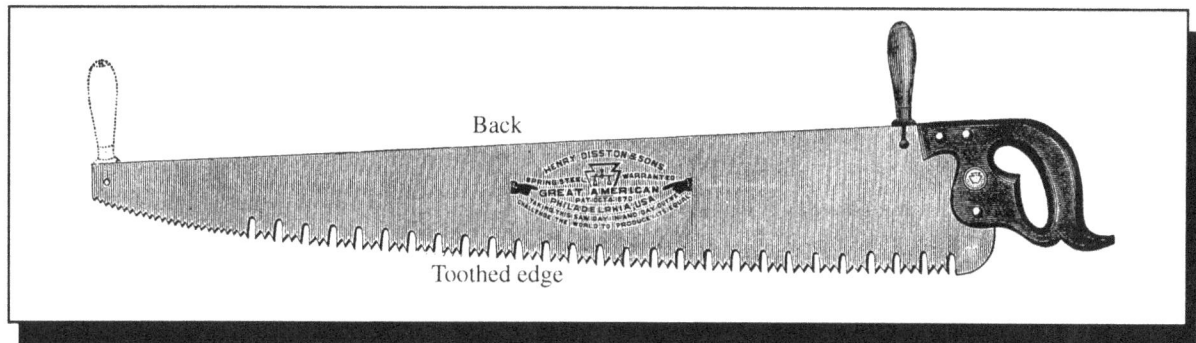

Figure 2—One-person crosscut saw. The handle can be placed in either of two locations on this vintage Disston saw. *—Henry Disston & Sons catalog (1902), with permission of Astragal Press, Mendham, NJ*

Two-Person Crosscut Saws

Two-person crosscut saws are symmetrical (figure 3). They cut in either direction. Two-person saws were 4 to 12 feet long for general sawing and up to 16 feet long for working in the California redwoods. If a longer saw was needed, two shorter saws were sometimes brazed together. Saws from 4 to 7 feet were made in ½-foot increments. Saws longer than 7 feet were made in 1-foot increments.

For felling, I try to select a saw that is twice the average diameter of the material I'll be sawing consistently. For bucking, I have found that it is easier and more efficient to use a shorter saw for an occasional large log than to carry a saw that is longer than I typically need.

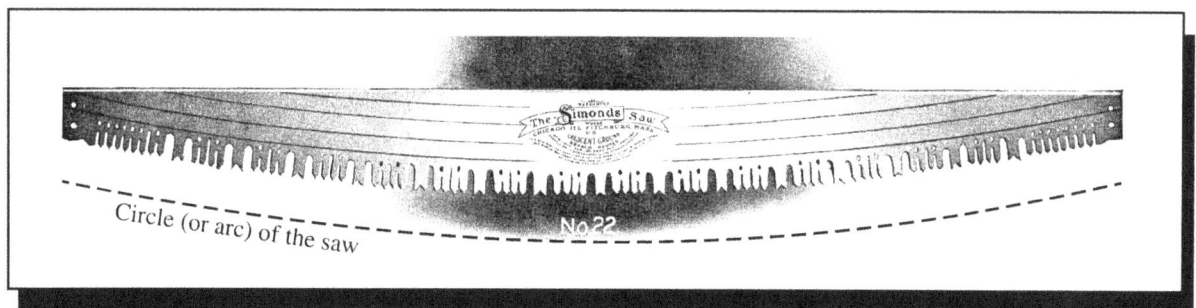

Figure 3—Two-person crosscut saw. *—Simonds, Inc., saws and knives catalog (1919), with permission of Roger K. Smith, Athol, MA*

Many vintage saws have teeth all the way to the ends, but saws manufactured today do not. I recommend using saws with teeth all the way to the end of the saw. This allows the greatest versatility for starting or ending a cut, for under-bucking, and for using a shorter saw.

Historically, two-person saws were manufactured with 15-gauge steel for the shorter 4- to 5-foot saws and a thicker 14-gauge for saws between 5 and 7 feet. Longer saws were typically 13-gauge. These thicknesses are measured at the tooth and represent the thickest metal in the saw. Straight taper and crescent taper saws were often a full 5 gauges thinner at the center back of the saw.

Felling Saws

Felling saws (figure 4) are best suited for felling standing timber. They cut best in a horizontal position. Felling saws have a concave back and are narrower than bucking saws. The combination of a concave back and narrower width give felling saws the following characteristics:

- The saw is more flexible.
- The saw is lighter, so less effort is needed to hold it horizontally.
- The saw has only one handle hole on each end.
- The sawyer can insert a wedge sooner.

The flexibility of the felling saw allows it to conform to the arc of the faller's arm. As the saw is pulled towards the sawyer, the saw rises, keeping it from binding. Historically, fallers standing on spring-boards (small platforms used to cut the tree) were able to transmit some of the energy from their legs into the saw much as you would if you rock forward on your toes when using a maul to split wood.

Because felling saws are limber and require two people to use them, they do not make good bucking or general all-around utility saws. I recommend instead that the bucking saw be the standard saw used for most trail and construction applications today.

Bucking Saws

Bucking saws (figure 4) have a straight back. They are thicker than felling saws, so they are heavier and stiffer. For example, my 6-foot Simonds 513 felling saw weighs 6¼ pounds, and my 6-foot Simonds 503 bucking saw weighs 8½ pounds.

Bucking saws can be used for occasional felling. Some saws were manufactured to incorporate the best characteristics of both felling and bucking saws.

I recommend the 5½-foot vintage bucking saw with teeth extending to the ends of the saw as the standard saw for most trail and construction applications today. This saw is used by a single sawyer.

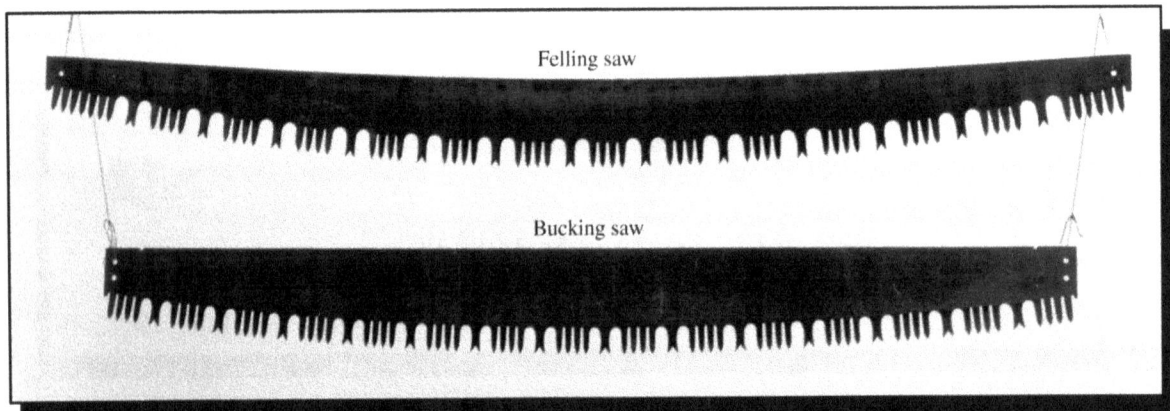

Figure 4—Felling saws have a curved back and often have just one handle hole per side. Straight-backed bucking saws often have two holes per side.

Sawyers need to master the skill of operating a two-person bucking saw solo before working with a partner as a bucking team. Because the bucking saw is usually operated by one person, it cuts on both the push and pull strokes. The saw's additional stiffness helps prevent the saw from buckling on the push stroke.

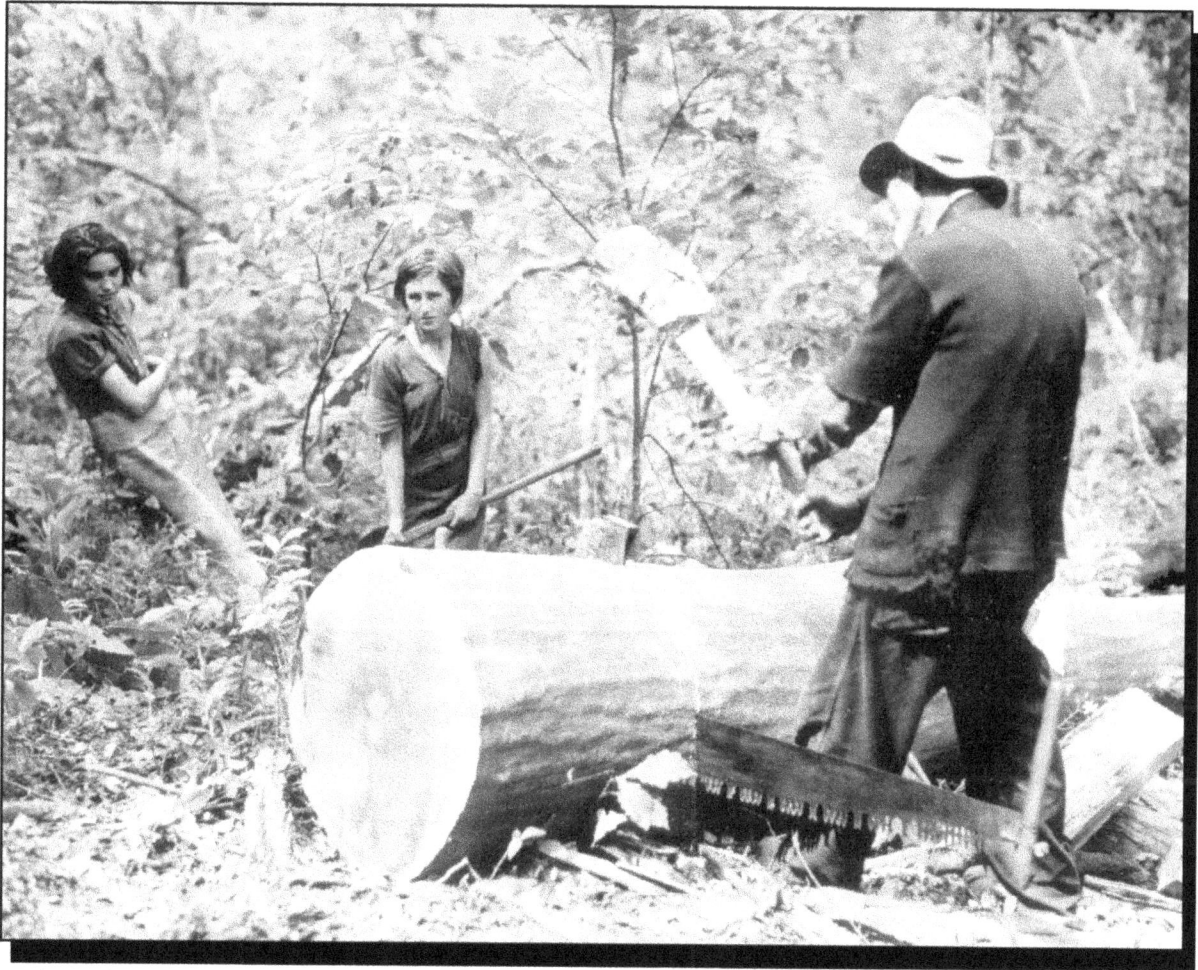

Appalachian family wedging a chestnut log, Tallulah Ranger District, Chattahoochee National Forest, Georgia.—*USDA Forest Service photo, date unknown*

Saw Grinds

The sides of vintage saws were finished, or ground, in three different ways. Each method affected the thickness of the saw in a particular way, and has major implications for the overall quality of the saw. These grinding methods are flat, straight taper, and crescent taper (figure 5).

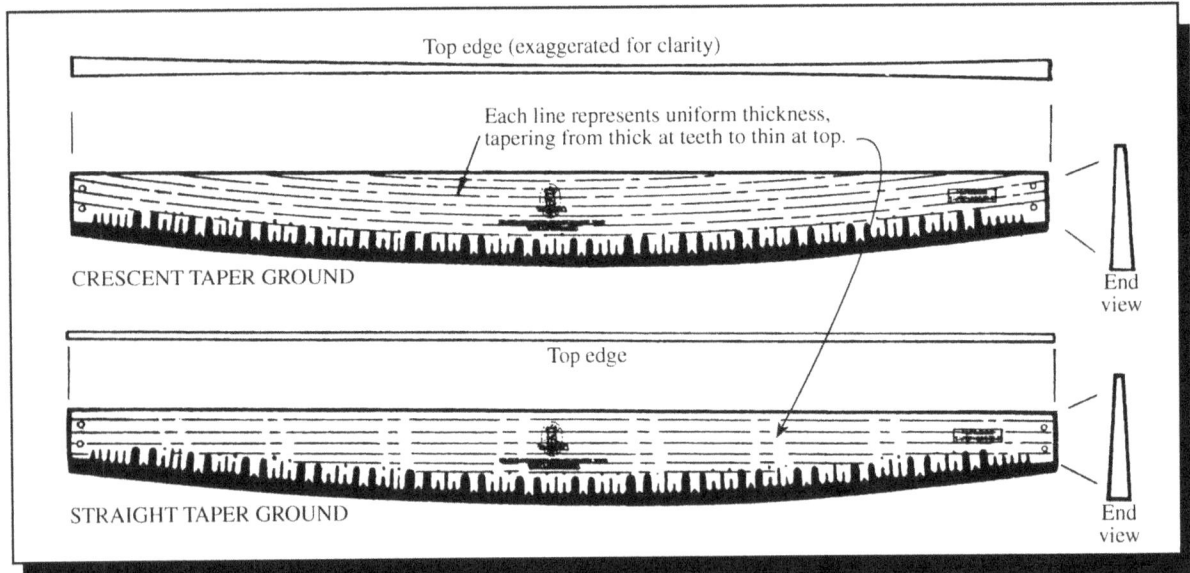

Top edge (exaggerated for clarity)

Each line represents uniform thickness, tapering from thick at teeth to thin at top.

CRESCENT TAPER GROUND

End view

Top edge

STRAIGHT TAPER GROUND

End view

Figure 5—A comparison of straight-taper-ground and crescent-taper-ground saws. Neither is manufactured today. Today's saws are flat ground, a design that is inferior to tapered saws.

Flat Ground

On a flat-ground saw, the metal's thickness is the same throughout. Saws manufactured today are flat ground.

Flat-ground saws are considered the least desirable. The main disadvantage is that it takes more set to enable the saw to clear the kerf (the slot the saw cuts in the wood). Set is the cutter tooth's offset from the plane of the saw. The kerf has to be wider for flat-ground saws, and more energy is required to use the saw (figure 6).

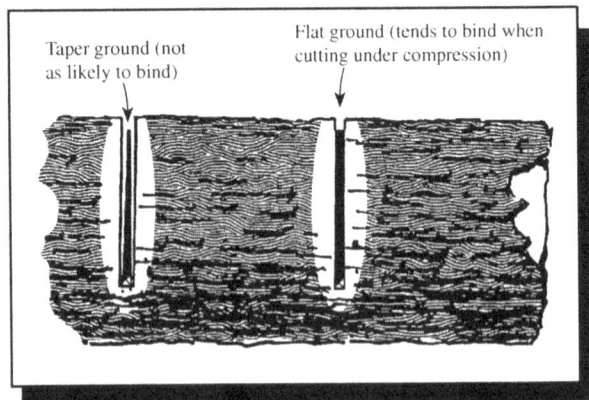

Taper ground (not as likely to bind)

Flat ground (tends to bind when cutting under compression)

Figure 6—A comparison between taper-ground and flat-ground saws. Taper-ground saws are less likely to bind.

Straight Taper Ground

Straight-taper-ground saws have an advantage over flat-ground saws because the saw is thinner at the back than at the teeth. The back of the saw has more clearance, reducing binding.

The teeth of straight-taper-ground saws are thicker near the center of the saw than along either end. Straight-taper-ground saws require less set than flat-ground saws.

Crescent Taper Ground

The best vintage saws were crescent taper ground. Warren Miller explains the difference between straight taper and crescent taper saws in the *Crosscut Saw Manual* (1977, rev. 2003): "The difference between the straight taper and crescent taper is that the lines of equithickness for the straight-taper-ground saw are straight and those for the crescent-taper-ground saw are concentric to the circle of the saw. This means that the teeth of the crescent-taper-ground saw are all the same thickness; whereas the teeth of the straight-taper-ground saw are thicker toward the center of the saw."

Crescent-taper-ground saws are no longer manufactured. They provide the maximum cutting efficiency with the least amount of human effort—the pinnacle of ergonomic design. They should be the best cared-for tool in the cache.

Saw manufacturing companies called crescent-taper-ground saws by different trade names: Crescent Ground (Simonds), Improved Ground (Disston), and Segment Ground (Atkins). Other names included Precision Ground and Arc Ground (figure 7).

Simonds Crescent Ground Cross-Cut Saws

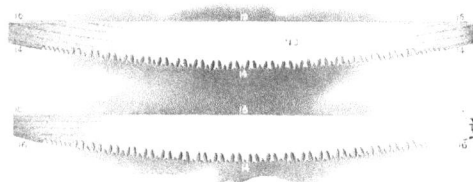

The Advantage

To grind Cross-Cut Saws in crescent lines parallel to the cutting edge of the saw is "Crescent Grinding." The advantage given by an even thickness throughout the tooth edge and a gradual taper from the tooth edge to the back is *less set* to the teeth and *less kerf* to cut. Our Crescent Ground Cross-Cut Saws have five gauges taper from the middle of the saw to the back, and two gauges taper from the ends of saw to the back.

No Binding in the Kerf

Note in the illustration of a *straight ground* saw the difference in

Figure 7—Companies like Simonds heavily promoted their Crescent Ground crosscut saws as the best ever made. The numbers refer to the gauge, or thickness, of the steel.—*Simonds saws and knives catalog (1919), with permission of Roger K. Smith, Athol, MA*

The thinnest part of a crescent ground saw is at the back center, which is often 4 or 5 gauges thinner than the teeth. If you hold one of these saws and sight down its back you can *see* the taper. You can *feel* the change in thickness (figure 5).

Crescent-taper-ground saws offer the saw the most clearance in the kerf of any of the grinds. These saws require the least amount of set, allowing the narrowest kerf.

How a Saw Cuts

The teeth of a saw function like a series of knives, making progressive simultaneous parallel cuts and releasing the wood between them (figure 8). These teeth perform three functions. They:

- Cut the wood fibers
- Break the cut fibers loose
- Remove the fibers from the kerf

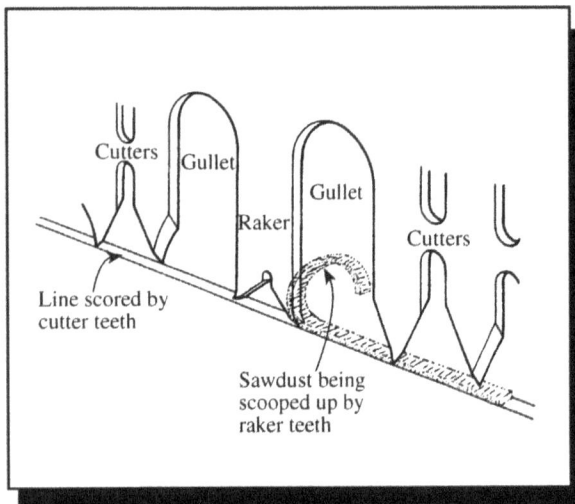

Figure 9—The configuration of the teeth of a crosscut saw. This is the perforated-lance tooth pattern.

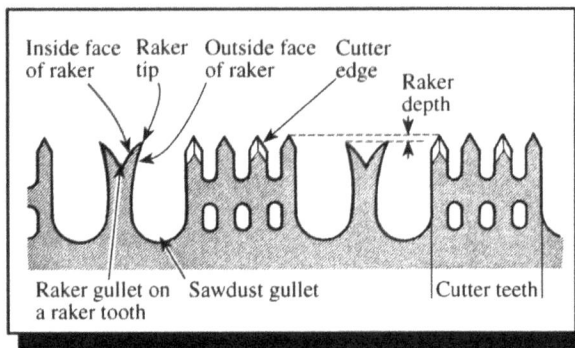

Figure 8—The way that the teeth of a crosscut saw work.—*Saws and Sawmills for Planters and Growers, with permission of John M. Morris*

Cutter Teeth

All saws, regardless of the tooth pattern, are made up of two rows of cutting edges. The saw releases wood fibers on each side of the kerf as it passes through a log. Cutters (figure 9) work best in brittle, seasoned wood. The weakened fiber is easily removed.

Rakers

Wet or green wood is hard to remove from the kerf because it is resilient. Even when the fiber is dislodged, it clogs a saw's cutter teeth.

A special kind of tooth, the raker, allows the cutter teeth to work more effectively with less effort. I prefer saws with rakers for general work in the woods.

Even though the rakers don't sever fiber, they perform the other two functions of saw teeth: breaking loose the cut

fiber and removing it from the log. Rakers remove material whether the saw is being pushed or pulled.

When rakers are shaped properly and their depth has been set accurately, they pull out long shavings of wood rather than sawdust (figure 10).

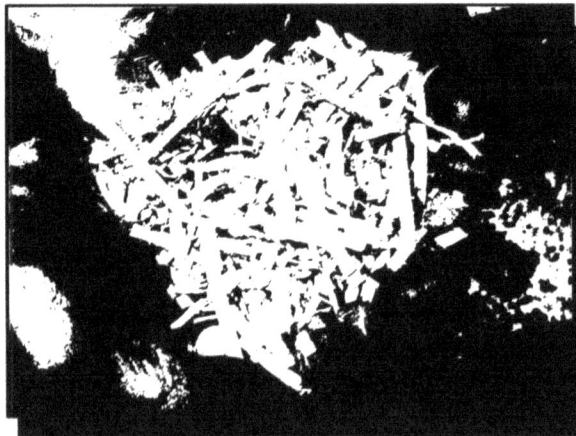

Figure 10—Long, clean shavings like these indicate a well-sharpened saw. In some parts of the country these shavings are called *noodles*.

Teeth That Both Cut and Rake

Some saws have teeth that both cut and rake. These teeth are asymmetrical (not uniform). One face is bevel filed to be the cutter while another face is filed almost flat to be the raker. The M tooth and Great American patterns are examples (figure 11). Teeth that are filed to both cut and rake are an improvement over the plain tooth in severing and removing wood fiber. However, these combination cutter-raker teeth

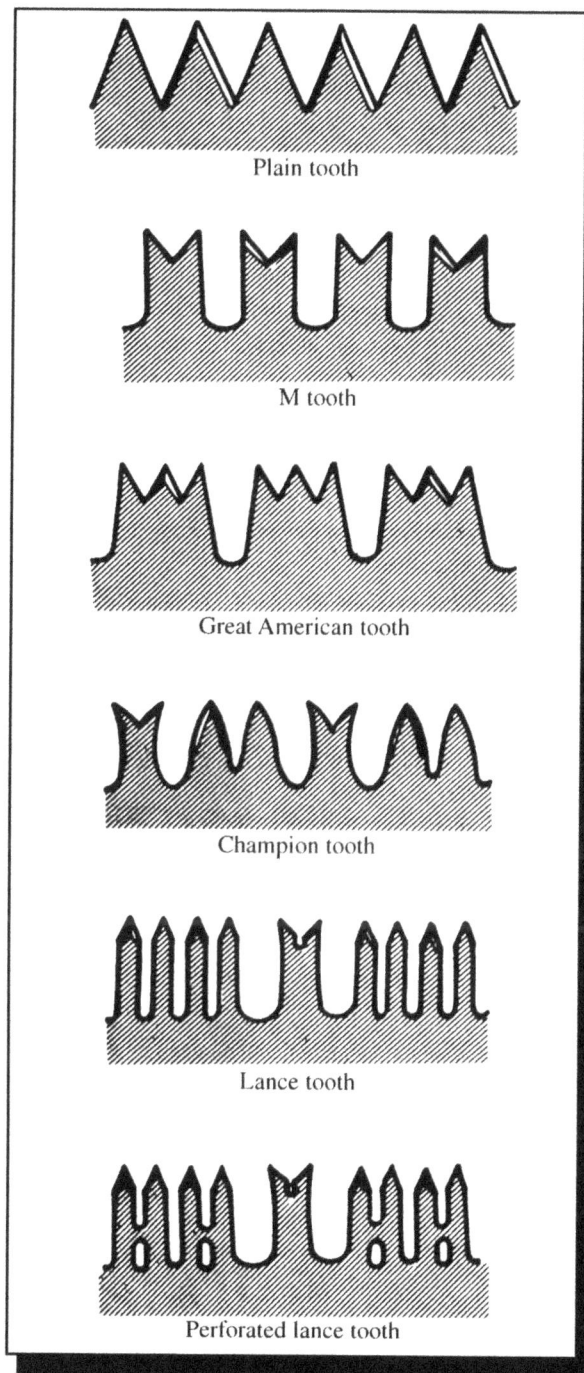

Figure 11—Common crosscut saw tooth patterns.

are a compromise. Without a raker to determine how far the tooth may penetrate, M tooth saws can cut very deeply and require a lot of strength to operate. While such an aggressive cutting action is appropriate for competition sawing, using such saws all day long for trail work is very fatiguing.

Gullets

Wood fiber that has been severed must be stored within the saw while the fiber is moved through the kerf. This storage area (the largest space between groups of cutters, or cutters and rakers) is called a gullet.

Gullets have a rounded shape so shavings will bend rather than break (figure 8). The gullet must be large enough to store all the shavings until the gullet clears the log and the shavings fall free. Saws that become worn out after repeated filings reduce the amount of shavings the gullet can hold.

The gullets determine the length of saw to use for a given application. For example, a gullet in the middle of a log 3 feet in diameter must travel $1\frac{1}{2}$ feet to allow its shavings to clear the log. At least a $6\frac{1}{2}$- or 7-foot saw would be needed to allow the shavings to clear a log 3 feet in diameter if the saw is being used by two persons. A shorter saw can be used by a single sawyer.

Tooth Spacing

The teeth of most crosscut saws lie on an arc of a circle (figure 3). This is sometimes called the circle of the saw, or the arc of the saw. This arc makes cutting faster, easier, and smoother. Especially on larger trees, when more teeth are being used, the arc causes the teeth to share the workload progressively instead of all at once. The circle of the saw works in conjunction with the arc of the sawyer's arm to effectively deliver power to the saw teeth as the saw feeds itself into the log.

The spacing of the saw's teeth ranks in importance with tooth pattern. Saw designers had to consider questions such as:

- Is the tooth strong enough for the intended work?
- Are the gullets far enough apart to effectively pick up all the fibers severed by the cutters?

- Is there enough room for the teeth and rakers to be sharpened and maintained?
- What's the best way to reduce vibration and chatter so the saw cuts smoothly?

The answer to these questions centers on tooth spacing. Generally, the longer the saw, the larger the teeth and the wider the space between teeth. Knowing tooth spacing helps the sawyer select the proper length of saw. Larger crosscut saws, with more space between the teeth, work poorly on small branches. Likewise, a small saw with small, closely spaced teeth doesn't work well on large trees or logs.

Tooth Patterns

For centuries, only the plain tooth (or peg tooth) pattern was used. Modifications to the plain tooth pattern were developed to make the saw easier to use. We will discuss six patterns: the plain tooth, the M tooth, the Great American tooth, the champion tooth, the perforated lance tooth, and the lance tooth.

Plain Tooth (Peg Tooth) Pattern

This pattern just includes cutter teeth. It is best used for cutting dry, very hard, or brittle small-diameter wood. Examples include many bow saws and pruning saws. These saws do not have special large gullets for sawdust. The sawdust is carried out in the small spaces between the teeth. Wet or resinous sawdust can bind up this tooth pattern.

M Tooth Pattern

The M tooth, still manufactured today in a modified form for competition saws, dates back to the 1400s in southern Germany. This tooth is designed to cut the fiber, break the severed fiber, and clean out the shavings. The tooth pattern consists of pairs of teeth set alternately and separated by a gullet. The outer edges of the teeth (the legs of the M) are vertical and act like rakers. The inside edges of the M are filed to a bevel, making a point. This tooth pattern is best suited for cutting dry, medium-to-hard woods.

Great American Tooth Pattern

This pattern consists of a group of three teeth, each set alternately, separated by a gullet. It is sometimes called a crown tooth because of its shape. The Great American tooth pattern is designed to cut dry, medium-to-hard woods. A special file is used for these saws. The file can be purchased today and is called a crosscut file or a Great American file. The file is shaped somewhat like a teardrop. The thicker rounded edge is for filing out the gullets. The sides of the file are used to file the rakers and cutters. This file also can be used to sharpen other tooth patterns.

Champion Tooth Pattern

This pattern is especially popular in the hardwood regions of North America. It consists of two cutter teeth set alternately and an unset raker with a gullet between them. The cutters are wider and more massive than the lance tooth pattern, allowing heavy sawing in extra hard, dry, or frozen wood. The larger teeth are sharpened in more of an almond shape rather than in the pointed shape of a lance tooth.

Lance Tooth Pattern

The lance tooth pattern also may be called the racer or four-tooth pattern. For many years the lance tooth pattern was the standard for felling and bucking timber in the American West. It consists of groups of four cutters set alternately, separated by an unset raker with gullets on each side. The lance tooth pattern is best suited for cutting soft green timber, especially fir, spruce, and redwood.

Perforated-Lance Tooth Pattern

This tooth pattern is considered a general utility pattern that can cut all but hard and frozen wood. It consists of groups of four cutters set alternately separated by an unset raker with gullets on each side. The "bridges" between the teeth form the perforations that give the pattern its name. These bridges strengthen the teeth and reduce chatter when the saw is used to cut harder wood. The perforated-lance tooth pattern is sometimes called the racer pattern and old-timers called it the four-tooth pattern. It was popular historically in the pine country of the American West, and is still popular there.

Saw Handles

The style, quality, and position of the handle on the saw greatly affect the saw's performance.

Types of Handles

Numerous designs have been used for saw handles. Many of these designs developed along regional preferences. Some were based on a particular saw's application. Many simply reflected the sawyer's preference as the most efficient way to transfer power from the sawyer's arms to the wood being cut.

Quality saw handles often are difficult to find. Handles must be strong and must not allow movement between the handle and the blade.

Handles may be fastened permanently to the blade with rivets (figure 12). These are rarely found and are usually removed so the saw can use pin-style handles. Removable handles may be fastened to the blade with a steel loop or with a pinned bolt and wing nut assembly. I prefer handles that are fastened with a pinned bolt and wing nut.

The handle's position on the saw affects the saw's efficiency. Changing either the arm and hand position, or the handle position, changes the delivery of force to the saw.

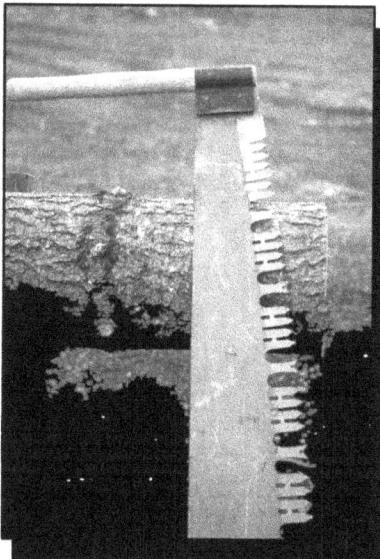

Figure 12—This vintage, but unused, Peugeot saw has its handles permanently fastened with rivets. The saw still has its original protective coating.

Loop-Style Handles

The loop-style handle is a common design (figure 13). Most of these models have a metal loop running up through a hardwood handle to a nut, which is either inside the handle (plug nut) or part of a cap at the end of the handle. The loop design allows the loop to be slipped over the saw blade. When the wooden handle is turned, the loop tightens around the saw. These models do not use the saw handle holes.

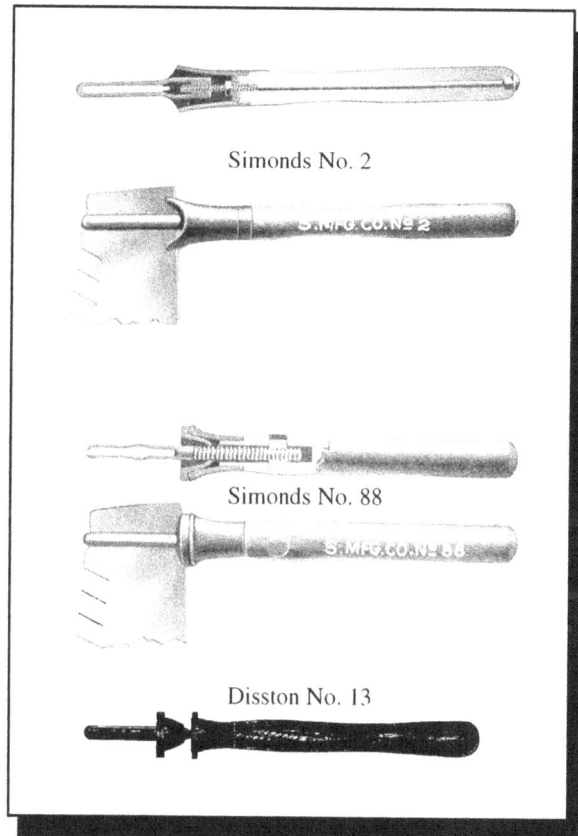

Simonds No. 2

Simonds No. 88

Disston No. 13

Figure 13—Examples of vintage loop-style handles.—*Henry Disston & Sons, Inc., catalog (1902), with permission of Astragal Press, Mendham, NJ; Simonds, Inc., saws and knives catalog (1919), with permission of Roger K. Smith, Athol, MA*

Many saws have a notch or a valley where the bottom of the loop rests. Because such saw blades must have a notch for the loop, they do not have teeth all the way to the end of the blade.

This saw and handle style is a disadvantage when I want to use just the end teeth to finish a cut. On the other hand, some sawyers like these models because the handle can be loosened and removed quickly with a twist of the wrist, an important safety factor in felling operations.

Another reason I dislike a loop handle is because most standard loop handles only allow the hands to be placed above the saw teeth. Occasionally you can find a vintage loop-style handle with a threaded bolt and wing nut. These handles offer both the quick removal of a loop-style handle and the good handle placement option of the pin-style handle. They have a long handle extending above and below the bracket, allowing the hands to be placed above or below the saw teeth.

Pin-Style Handles

The pin-style handle design—the most common—uses handle holes in the saw blade.

Climax-style handles were an inexpensive pin-style design. Even today, they appear on some modern two-person crosscut saws (figure 14). Logging companies bought climax-style handles because they were inexpensive, but sawyers did not like them. Often I see pins damaged to the point that these handles cannot be removed from the saw blade. The damage results from sawyers tightening down too hard on the wing nut (often with a pair of pliers), as they try to reduce movement between the handle and the blade.

A pin that is too small in diameter, or made of a metal that is too soft also may cause damage. These handles do not allow the hands to be placed above or below the attachment, so I do not use them.

Perhaps the most common vintage saw handle used today is the Pacific Coast model of the pin-style design (figure 15). It has a finger guard with a groove to accept the saw blade and two cast flanges that saddle the wooden handle. The $\frac{1}{2}$-inch-diameter bolt passes through a hole in the wooden handle. It is secured with a heavy wing nut. This allows the long end of the handle to be placed above or below the pin.

Some sawyers today do not like this style of handle because they prefer to place their hand where the bolt end and wing nuts are located. I find there is no real need to have my hands over the bolt. These pin-style handles are my preference for general trail-clearing and felling operations.

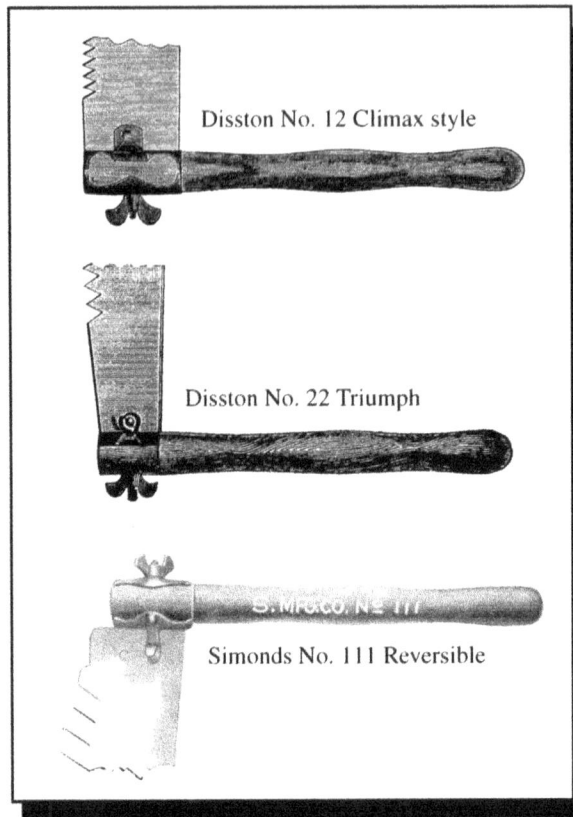

Figure 14—Pin-style handle designs.—*Henry Disston & Sons, Inc., catalog (1902), with permission of Astragal Press, Mendham, NJ; Simonds saws and knives catalog (1919), with permission of Roger K. Smith, Athol, MA*

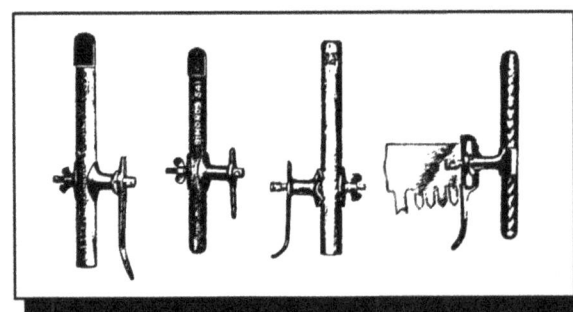

Figure 15—Pacific Coast model of the pin-style handle. This type is my personal favorite for general trail clearing and felling.

Standard 14-inch bucking handles had the bolt hole $5\frac{1}{2}$ inches from the end of the handle. This allowed the sawyer to choose to mount the handle with either the short or long portion up.

Some pin-style saw handles are called *reversible* or *universal* (figure 14). They were designed to allow the sawyer to rotate the handle, to keep the handle vertical whether felling, top cutting, or undercutting.

Supplementary handles (figure 16) are used on one-person crosscut saws. The handle can be placed on the end of the saw for an additional sawyer or directly in front of the D-shaped handle when a single sawyer wants to use both hands. I recommend having one of these available.

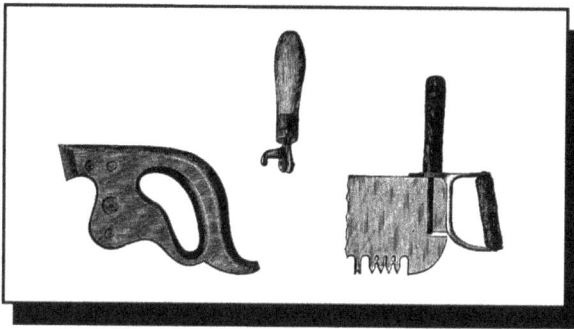

Figure 16—One-person saw "D" handle and supplemental handles from a vintage Disston catalog.—*Henry Disston & Sons, Inc., catalog (1902), with permission of Astragal Press, Mendham, NJ*

Because the handle is so important to a saw's efficiency, I use only vintage handles, or their reproductions. Until recently, no one was making any of the original saw handle designs. In 1990, a foundry started producing a replica of a popular West Coast design similar to an Atkins No. 140 handle (see the Sources section). Vintage handles are still preferred by crosscut saw users.

Handle Installation and Maintenance

A one-person saw has a fixed D-shaped handle with additional holes on the top of the saw where a supplemental handle can be attached. Many two-person crosscut saws (usually bucking saws) have two holes on each end for handles. Moving the handle from the lower hole has the same effect as moving the hands several inches up the saw handle. With the handle in the upper hole, a push stroke applies more downward force on the saw, causing the teeth to sink deeper into the wood. The deeper cut requires more force on the push stroke, but applies a slight upward force on the pull stroke.

The wooden handles on crosscut saws are usually select-grade hardwoods $1\frac{1}{4}$ inches in diameter and about 14 inches long. Felling saws often had shorter handles with the mounting bolt hole drilled in the center of the handle. When the handle is not on the saw, it needs to be kept away from sharp edges that could nick or cut it.

It's important to keep the wooden handle sanded smooth and to keep it well oiled with boiled linseed oil. Sand off any lacquered finish before applying the oil.

Keep metal parts of handles free of rust. To recondition old handles, I soak the metal parts in penetrating oil and brush them with a wire brush. If rusted wing nuts cannot be removed, sacrifice the wing nut rather than the machined threaded bolt. I use a torch to heat just the nut, expanding it so I can remove it. If that doesn't work, cut the nut off with a hacksaw. Use a thread chaser to touch up the threads and purchase a new malleable iron wing nut. Thin, cheap wing nuts are not suitable.

If I need replacement pins, I use a quality steel rivet of similar diameter. These rivets can be obtained from a good industrial supply house. The slotted mounting bolt is designed to hold the rivet when the saw is not attached. One side of the bolt has a smaller diameter hole than the other. I place the new rivet through the entire bolt. Then I slightly peen the end of the rivet to enlarge it. The rivet now should pass through the large end of the slotted bolt but not be able to fall completely out.

Saw Maintenance

These maintenance topics are intended for the crosscut sawyer. Some topics, such as saw filing, are included just to provide an overview. An experienced saw filer should actually do the filing. The *Crosscut Saw Manual* by Warren Miller (1977, rev. 2003) is a resource for more information on saw maintenance and filing.

I cannot overemphasize the need to have saws professionally sharpened. I continue to see quality vintage saws being used as "misery whips" because they were not properly sharpened.

Cleaning the Saw

Saws need to be clean to function effectively. Clean saws at the end of the day before storing them.

The goal is to remove all deposits on the surface of the saw without causing any damage. When saws have not been properly cared for over a long time, permanent damage can occur.

To clean the saw, remove the handles and place the saw on a flat wooden surface that you don't mind getting oily. I made a special beam table for cleaning saws. I took a smooth 8-by-8 timber 8 feet long and countersunk a number of magnets below the surface to hold the saw in place. These thin round magnets are sold as *pot magnets* at industrial supply houses. They have a hole in the center so they can be mounted with a screw. Place the beam on top of a couple of sawhorses that are about 30 to 36 inches high. Place the saw on the beam.

Rust causes more damage to saws than anything else. A wire brush can be used to remove loose rust and scale. Never use a power sanding disk on a saw blade. Remove light rust using steel wool. Normally, I use fine grade (No. 0) steel wool for saw work, although coarser grades are sometimes needed.

Use a pumice grill block to remove rust that is too heavy to be removed with steel wool. Pumice grill blocks are brick shaped (about 4 by 4 by 8 inches) and are used to clean grill tops. They can be bought at a restaurant supply house. Take long sweeping strokes with the stone back and forth along the length of the blade while you are standing over the saw. A liberal amount of cleaning solution or water will keep the block's pores open.

Don't apply too much pressure on the cutter teeth because you can remove metal from the set and shorten the teeth.

To remove heavier rust, use an ax stone. Always use a liberal amount of cleaning solution, either oil or water, depending on the stone. Never use a dry stone on the saw blade.

As rust is removed, the saw begins to tell a story. Sometimes you can see the original acid etching revealing the saw manufacturer and the name and model of the saw.

The manufacturer's etching may be destroyed over time, so you should be careful not to rub it out during cleaning. As a safeguard, I use an electric etcher to record the manufacturer and model number near the handle. I also assign the saw a number and etch the number and the name of the USDA Forest Service administrative unit on the blade. Keep a paper record describing the general amount of use and the sharpening record, such as the date of sharpening, raker depth, and tooth set.

As rust and other deposits are removed, you will see imperfections in the saw blade. Shiny spots indicate high spots. Spots that are duller than the normal saw surface indicate low spots. A high spot on one side of the blade usually produces a low spot on the other side. These kinks or bends need to be hammered out by an experienced saw filer.

Cleaning Solutions

Field Cleaning

A saw that is well cared for will not rust, but it will develop pitch deposits during normal use. Some pitch can be removed with a citrus-based solvent as the saw is being used. The saw's motion scrubs away the buildup. Traditionally, kerosene was used to clean the saw, but it is not recommended today because of environmental concerns and potentially harmful health effects.

Even when the saw is being lubricated, pitch can be deposited on the saw. Pitch buildups can be removed at the end of the day with steel wool and a cleaning solution.

Limit the use of harsh chemicals in remote settings where it may be difficult to handle such products properly.

Shop Cleaning

Harsher chemical products may be used in a shop, but only if you have access to proper disposal and handling methods.

Wear the proper personal protective equipment and know how to use the cleaning solutions safely. Check the Material Safety Data Sheet (MSDS) if you are unfamiliar with the hazards of using and storing a particular product. A number of citrus-based cleaners on the market are effective and are safer than petroleum-based solvents. Citrus-based cleaners are recommended rather than the traditional cleaners because they are safer to use and less harmful to the environment. The cleaning agents should not be left on the saw for long periods.

Generally speaking, rust and pitch can be removed by dissolving the deposits and wiping the saw clean or by abrasion.

Diesel fuel is both a solvent and an oil, so it was traditionally used with a stone or pumice block to clean saws. Another product often used for cleaning was kerosene or Jet-A fuel. Kerosene worked better for dissolving pitchy surfaces and was historically the solvent of choice.

A solution of muriatic acid (a commercial grade of hydrochloric acid) worked well on heavily pitted saws. Soap and hot water with a degreaser like TSP (trisodium phosphate) or Spic-n-Span also removes pitch.

A plastic squeeze bottle is a good container for applying cleaners in the shop. The squeeze bottle is just for applying the solution, not for storage. These products must be stored in an approved container.

Naval gel can be applied to remove heavy rust and scale. Use only as directed, with adequate ventilation. This product stops the chemical reaction of the rust.

Checking for Straightness

A saw should be checked for straightness if it receives any harsh treatment during transportation or use. A saw that is not straight can buckle on the push stroke. Additionally, a saw that is not straight will not cut efficiently. The narrower, lighter felling saws are most prone to buckling.

Using Straightedges

Remove the saw's handles and hang the saw from one of its handle holes. You will need a pair of straightedges. Saw filers usually have straightedges made especially for this work, available from sawmill supply companies (figure 17). Two combination square rules can be used. Two 12- or 18-inch metal drafting straightedges also work well. Before using the straightedges on the saw, hold them together and make sure they maintain contact along their entire length. You should not see light between them when you put them together and hold them up to a light source.

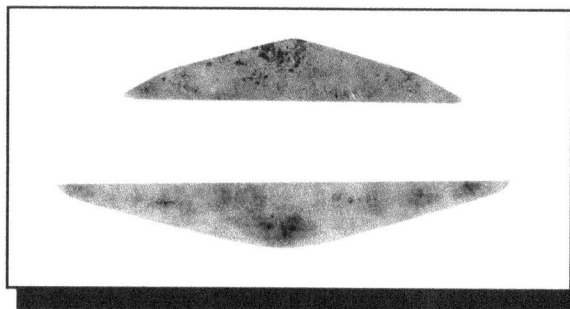

Figure 17—Examples of sawmaker's straightedges.

Straightedges work by allowing you to feel the difference in resistance between the saw and the straightedge as they are twisted back and forth over the saw's surface. Holding one straightedge in each hand, move the straightedges as a pair with the saw between them. You will feel increased drag on the ends of the straightedge on the side of a saw with a depression. On the other side of the saw, the straightedge will pivot easily on the corresponding bump. Even resistance on both straightedges indicates a straight saw that does not have any kinks, bends, or bumps (figure 18).

If you find any major irregularities, mark them and tell the person who files your saws.

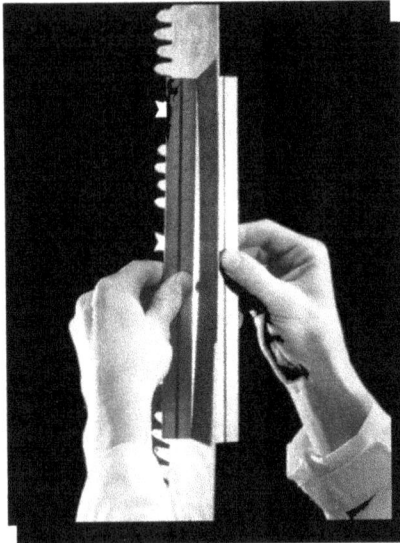

Figure 18—Locating kinks with two straightedges.

Often, a saw that needs straightening may be used until the next sharpening. However, the saw is more susceptible to buckling and will not cut as effectively. I don't recommend bending a saw that has a known irregularity so it can be transported. Such bending can compound the problem.

Testing the Saw

Testing determines whether a saw cuts straight, runs smooth, and produces long, thick shavings. The saw should produce shavings, not sawdust. The longer and more abundant the shavings, the better the saw is performing. Green logs produce longer shavings than dry logs. The shavings should be long and thick with smooth edges. If the edges of the shavings have "whiskers" or irregularities, the rakers are probably too long. If the shavings are paper thin, the rakers are too short (figure 19).

Tooth patterns without separate rakers (plain, M tooth, and Great American) usually do not produce long shavings, but produce chunky shavings with some sawdust.

Does the saw cut straight? Cut far enough into the test log to determine whether the cut is perfectly straight. Sometimes a sawyer standing in an awkward position can put a twist or bend on the saw that causes it to cut crooked.

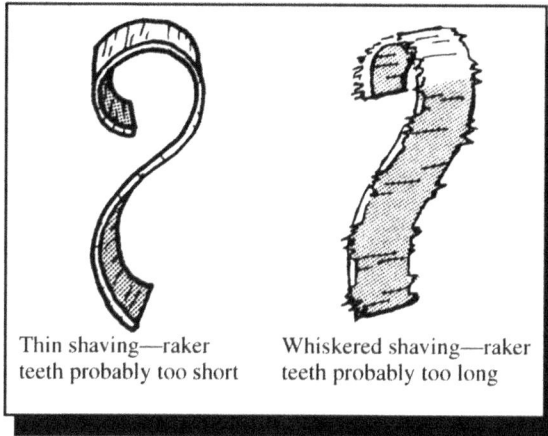

Thin shaving—raker teeth probably too short   Whiskered shaving—raker teeth probably too long

Figure 19—Examining shavings to identify sharpening problems.

However, if the saw consistently pulls to one side through no fault of the sawyer, the saw needs additional maintenance.

A saw will not cut straight if it is kinked or bent. Too much set on one side of the cutters can cause the saw to pull to that side. If a saw has been sharpened improperly, the teeth may be longer on one side than the other. The saw will pull to the side with the longer teeth.

Never field sharpen or touch up dull cutters. Doing so shortens the teeth, compounding the problem.

Does the saw run smooth? The saw may feel like it is alternately catching and releasing. A smooth-running saw, on

A sharp vintage saw runs so smoothly that it is said to "sing." Such a saw is well tuned. Sadly, many crosscut sawyers have neither heard nor experienced the joy of working with a well-tuned saw.

the other hand, seems to cut effortlessly. Look for a saw that doesn't chatter or seem like it is jumping as it cuts through the log.

Smoothness is most associated with the rakers. If a saw feels like it is snagging the wood, it is probably because one or more rakers have been filed incorrectly.

Inconsistent set in the teeth also can produce a jumpy saw. Look at the walls of the cut. A well-tuned crosscut saw leaves a smooth cut surface.

A cutter that has too much set may cause a saw to run rough. The saw may feel like there is a slight check or pause followed by a little jump.

A sawyer cannot do anything to fix a saw that is running rough. A qualified saw filer needs to make the necessary adjustments. Describe the problems to the filer.

Saw Filing

Good filers are few and far between. The filer's work is exacting and requires a lot of stamina and patience. Back in 1939, George C. Parker wrote in the *West Coast Lumberman*: "*There is today a scarcity of crosscut saw filers. This dearth of filers has gradually made itself manifest during the past 10 years. Filers are not made overnight. Years of practical experience are necessary before they become skilled and efficient.*"

Today, crosscut saw filers are much scarcer than they were in 1939. Treat any you know with respect, but insist on excellence in the work they perform. Ask them the number of saws they sharpen each year—more is better. Avoid filers who recommend only one setting for all types of cutting conditions. Our traditional crosscut saws cut well only when they are sharpened properly. The sawyer needs to tell the filer the expected cutting conditions. For example, cutting green blowdown in winter requires different raker and teeth set than cutting dry, beetle-killed snags. It is important to communicate this information to the filer.

The lack of qualified filers is as important as the shortage of good saws in eventually relegating crosscut saws to curio shops and collectors' shelves instead of their rightful role as working tools in the woods.

A few others and I are working with saw designers to create a saw that not only meets our trail clearing needs, but also can be sharpened by using a simple jig. Such a design is technically possible, though it is unlikely this type of saw would cut as well as a well-tuned vintage crosscut saw.

The *Crosscut Saw Manual* by Warren Miller (1977, rev. 2003) is a source of information on filing. Another publication is *Saws and Sawmills for Planters and Growers* by John Morris (1991).

It is important for the crosscut saw user to understand the skill and labor required to sharpen and recondition a saw. You will be more inclined to take care of your saws and to keep them from getting dull if you know how much work it takes to sharpen them.

Saw Vises and Tools

A filer needs to work in a well-lit location with a wooden vise that sandwiches the saw to hold it firm. I prefer vises that are heavy and massive rather than those that are lightweight and flimsy.

Specialized saw tools that every filer used to have are no longer being manufactured. Some replicas are being made, but vintage saw tools are superior. Anderson Tools are truly antiques and would be difficult to replace if lost or damaged. Files and sharpening stones are readily available, but tools like jointers, raker and pin gauges, anvils, and swaging hammers are scarce.

Straightening

Straightening is an art in itself. The filer must move the metal carefully by hammering the blade on an anvil. A special saw filer's hammer has slightly curved surfaces to work the metal back into place. I have sometimes spent more time trying to get a saw straight than I have spent sharpening it (figure 20).

Jointing

After the saw has been cleaned and straightened, jointing is the first step in sharpening. A tool called a jointer holds the file. The points are filed off the cutter tips so that each of them lies on the circle of the saw (figure 21). With each of the teeth lightly touched, this arc will become the reference plane for fitting rakers and sharpening teeth.

Figure 20—Hammering out a kink using a specially shaped saw hammer.

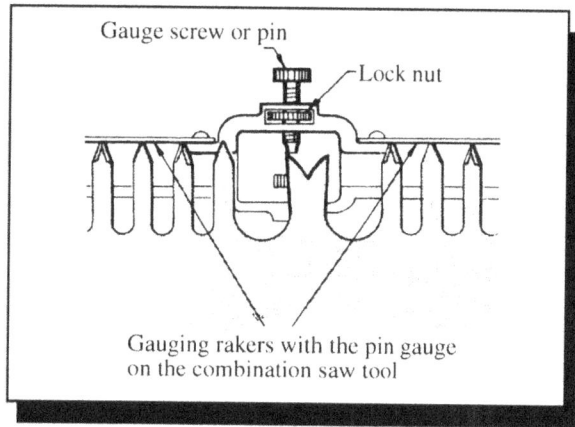
Figure 22—Gauging rakers.

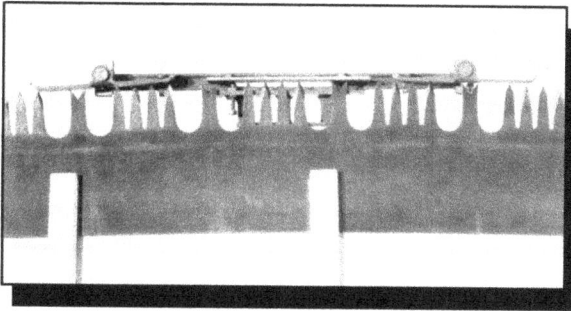
Figure 21—Jointing a saw with a long jointer, the preferred tool.

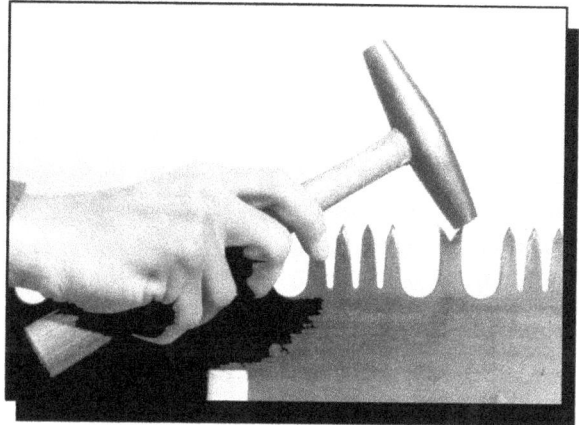
Figure 23—Striking the inside face of the raker tip with a hammer.

Fitting Rakers

I use a triangular file to shape the raker gullet. A raker gauge is placed on top of the cutters that have already been jointed to form the reference plane. With the rakers sticking up through the gauge, the rakers are filed down to a predetermined stop. Swedged rakers are fitted differently. They are hammered to a pin gauge (figures 22 and 23).

Tooth Pointing

Each tooth is sharpened to a point (figure 24). The filer has the option to make the bevel suit the wood that is being cut. It is very important that all the teeth are the same height in relationship to the rakers (figure 25).

Setting Teeth

The teeth need to be set so they track directly behind one another in a measured angle offset from vertical. The filer

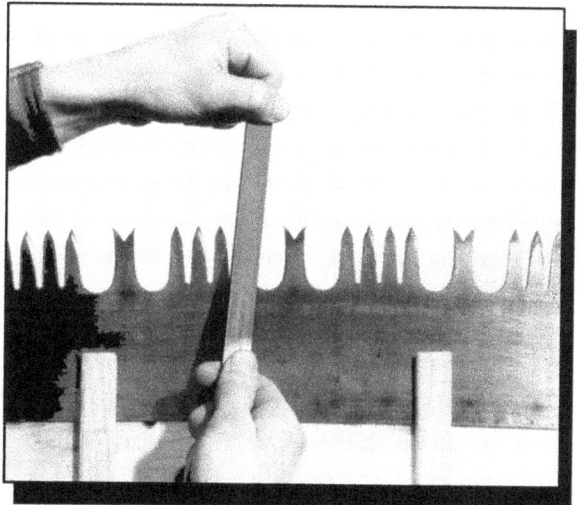
Figure 24—Filing a cutter tooth.

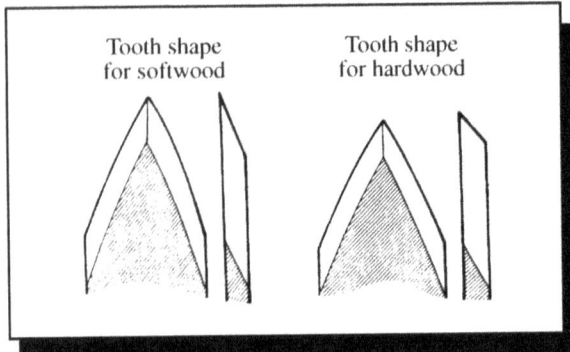

Figure 25—Shapes of crosscut saw teeth. Bevels can be adjusted to best suit the wood being cut.

puts equal set in all the teeth by hammering the point over a beveled hand anvil (figure 26). The set is checked using a tool called a spider to tolerances of $5/_{1,000}$ of an inch.

After setting the teeth, I side-hone them to further ensure they all have the same set. I recommend this procedure even though it is not commonly mentioned in saw sharpening literature.

A final word about filing—If saws consistently come back from the filer but do not run smoothly and *sing*...find another filer.

Figure 26—Warren Miller setting cutter teeth.

Storage

Whether crosscut saws are stored at a backcountry guard station or in the district warehouse, they need to be stored properly.

Long-Term Storage

Store crosscut saws straight. Remove the handles and store the saws in a dry location.

Never store a saw flat on a metal surface. Although the saw can be laid horizontally if it is supported along its entire length, items may be dropped on a saw, damaging it. It is best to hang a saw from a nail through a handle hole.

Store the saw with a coating of heavy oil or grease diluted with solvent. The coating needs to be thick enough that it will not evaporate. Plant-based lubricants like canola oil are not appropriate coatings for long-term storage. These oils dry out and leave a hard residue on the saw that is difficult to remove.

Near saltwater environments, wash your saws in clean water to remove any salt residue before applying the heavy oil coating. Wear gloves when applying the oil.

Never lean a saw against a wall where the saw could develop a bend. Never leave a saw bent around a fire pack.

Do not store a saw in a sheath or with a guard on the blade. Rubber-lined firehose is particularly bad because it holds moisture next to the saw's teeth. If the teeth become pitted, the saw is useless because damaged teeth will not withstand the hammering needed during sharpening.

Do not hang a saw where people or animals could be injured by the unsheathed teeth. Do not store saws on top of one another. When the unsheathed saws rub against each other, the saws can be damaged.

I prefer to store my saws unsheathed on 16d finishing nails driven into the top plate of a wall in an isolated area of a building, where the saws do not present a hazard. Use 3-inch square pieces of corrugated cardboard as spacers between saws hanging on the same nail.

Storage in the Field

Moisture forms rust, and rust ruins saws, so take every effort to keep the saw dry. Saws can't always be kept dry in the field, so I place wet saws where they will dry quickly. Try hanging the saw under a heavily limbed tree where the branches will help protect it, or on the side of the tree that exposes the saw to the sun or wind. Remove the saw's sheath before drying, and tie the saw so it will not blow around in the wind.

Once the saw is dry, wipe it clean and rub it with an oily rag. Choose a storage location out of sight and away from game trails.

Remove the saw handles and sheath. Bears tend to gnaw on wooden handles. Rodents chew on leather straps and anything that has salt on it. Leave nothing but the metal parts in the field. If the saw is only being left overnight, it can be stored under a log with the teeth pointed in. If you are storing a saw longer than for just one night, hang it.

Saw Sheaths

Sheaths protect the saw and prevent it from causing damage or inflicting injury. Saws should be sheathed as much as possible unless they are being used or are in storage. Wear gloves whenever you remove or replace a saw sheath.

Saw sheaths can be rigid or flexible. Rigid sheaths are easier for hikers to carry for long distances because the saw blade doesn't flop up and down on the hiker's shoulder. One sawyer told me that his saw broke while he carried it over his shoulder. I assume the constant flexing led to metal fatigue.

Rigid sheaths can cover just the saw's teeth or the entire blade. Flexible sheaths provide protection while allowing saws to be bent around backpacks or over pack animals. Flexible sheaths also are lightweight and easier to carry when they are not on the saw.

A length of old firehose that has been split makes one of the best crosscut saw sheaths. Wipe the hose's rubber inner lining with an oily rag to repel water and reduce the possibility that moisture in the sheath will cause the saw to rust. Sheaths made of leather and nylon are available commercially. The Missoula Technology and Development

Center (MTDC) also has come up with a design for a saw sheath (figure 27, see *Crosscut Saw Guards* by George Jackson, 1997).

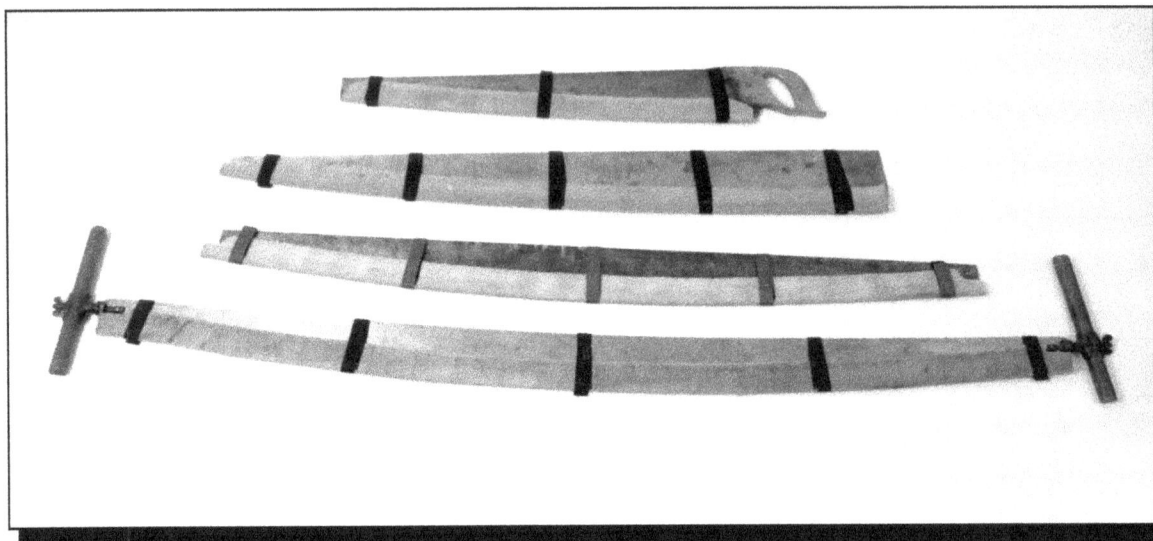

Figure 27—MTDC developed this saw sheath. The guard is made from 1½-inch discarded firehose using nylon straps and hook-and-loop fasteners.

Wear gloves to install the hose sheath. Begin by rolling the sheath inside out (rubber side out). Turn the saw so its teeth face up; unroll the hose down the saw, covering the teeth (figure 28). Attach the sheath to the saw using parachute cord or Velcro closures.

Some sawyers sandwich the saw between two rectangular pieces of plywood. The saw's handle holes are placed over pins at each end of one of the pieces of plywood, securing the saw.

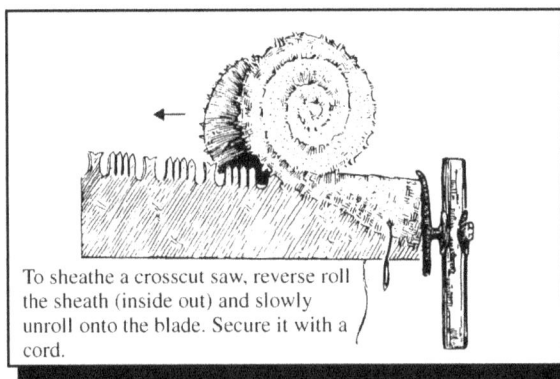

To sheathe a crosscut saw, reverse roll the sheath (inside out) and slowly unroll onto the blade. Secure it with a cord.

Figure 28—The proper way to unroll rubber-lined firehose onto a saw. Wear gloves to protect your hands.—*Copyright 1996. Reprinted with permission of the publisher of Robert C. Birkby's Lightly on the Land, published by the Student Conservation Association and The Mountaineers, Seattle, WA*

Transporting Saws

Saws that are being transported must be handled so they will not be damaged, so they will not injure people or livestock, and so they will not damage property and equipment.

Saws are difficult to transport because they are long and flexible. Vintage saws can be bent to make them easier for hikers or packstock to carry. You will not want to bend a vintage saw that has a nick or is not straight. Modern saws should not be bent. The softer metal will hold the bend, ruining the saw.

Because saws may be carried by a hiker, taken by boat, plane, helicopter, truck, dog sled, or packstock, or even be dropped by parachute during different legs of a journey, several types of protection may be needed. Sheaths should always cover saws when they are being transported.

Saws get hot in the sun. Be especially careful to wear gloves when handling a saw that has been lying in the sun. Also, gloves can prevent the cuts that would otherwise occur when you are putting on and taking off the saw sheath.

Boats

Particularly in Alaska, crosscut saws may be carried in boats. When a saw is carried as general cargo in large boats, it should be sandwiched between plywood and laid flat, if possible. In open skiffs, where space limitations preclude using a rigid plywood sheath, remove the saw's handles and place the saw on top of other cargo with only the teeth sheathed. On many boats, the saw may be kept out of the way if it is stored along the gunwales.

Open boats can take on a lot of spray. Saltwater spray can cause rust. Once the saw is on land, remove the sheath and rinse off any salt with freshwater.

Saws transported on kayaks are best secured to the bow, where they can be seen. In canoes, carry saws in the center on the floor. Transport the saw without handles in a rubber-lined hose sheath. Secure the saw by tying parachute cord through the handle holes and tying the cord to the canoe or kayak.

Aircraft

In small aircraft, firehose sheaths will allow the best flexibility so the saw can fit in tight quarters. Cargo and passengers must be separated, often by a nylon net. Sometimes the sheathed saw can lie flat. At other times, the saw needs to be bent into a loop. Normally, when a saw is bent, the handles are left on and tied together. In small aircraft, the handles often get in the way. If so, remove the handles, bend the saw into a loop, and secure the saw ends of the saw with **wire** through the handle holes.

Do not string parachute cord or any other nonmetallic material (including nylon ties) through a saw's handle holes to secure it for transport in a plane or helicopter. Jostling during the flight could cut nonmetallic materials, allowing the saw to spring to full length. What might happen to passengers or an aluminum cargo compartment is best left to your imagination.

When carrying saws aboard helicopters, crewmembers must exercise great care to ensure the saws do not stick up into the helicopter rotor.

Saws also can be transported by helicopters in external sling loads. External loads are carried in cargo nets, bags, or slings. If other pieces of rigid cargo are as long as the saw, the saw, sandwiched in plywood, can be secured to them.

When saws are tied in a loop, they are prone to damage or breakage. Bending the saw around a solid object is better than bending it around a soft object, such as a duffel bag. One way to reduce breakage is to bend the saw around a box. Place the box in the middle of the sling bag with the saw's ends down. Stack other materials around the saw, being careful to avoid a box at the top that could shift, applying pressure to the bend. The saw should be relatively safe unless the load tips over on landing.

Parachutes have long been used to deliver saws for firefighting. Because the bent saw is exposed during the landing, good vintage saws occasionally are broken (figure 29).

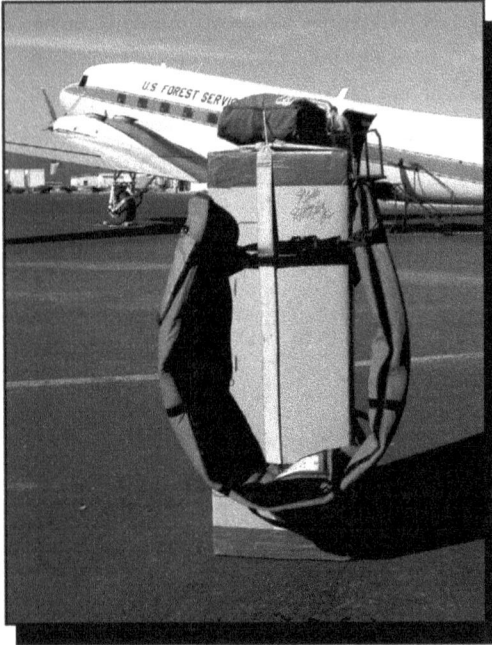

Figure 29—A crosscut saw rigged for a parachute drop.

Vehicles

When transporting crosscut saws in a pickup truck, lay the sheathed saw flat on the bed of the truck, preferably on a truck bed liner rather than on the steel bed. Don't place heavy tools on top of the saw. Do not carry saws in the passenger compartment of a vehicle.

Packstock

Be extra careful when carrying a crosscut saw on packstock. Select the gentlest animal to carry the saw. Put that animal in the lead where you can easily see the saw. Leave the handles attached to a two-person saw. The heads of the rivet attachment pins should face up, not down, so the pins won't slide out and cause the handles to fall off. Covering both sides of the pins with strips of duct tape gives further assurance the pins won't slide out. Sheathe the saw with firehose. Some packers wrap the saw in a separate mantie (canvas cover used to wrap loads) with the handles secure and exposed. Bend the saw and place it over the animal. Some pack the saw with the teeth facing the rear of the animal to minimize the likelihood of injury if the sheath falls off. Others pack the saw

with the longest end of the handles pointing to the back, where they are less likely to get caught on trailside branches. Go with what works best for you considering the trail conditions you will be facing. Tie the saw handles down to the latigo or cinch ring (figure 30). Also tie the center of the bowed saw with a rope that goes to the front sawbuck or the "D" ring of a Decker saddle. It's important to secure the bowed saw to the packsaddle and not just to the load. With the saw fastened on top, it is more likely the saw will stay on top of the animal and not fall to the side if the rope on either side becomes untied.

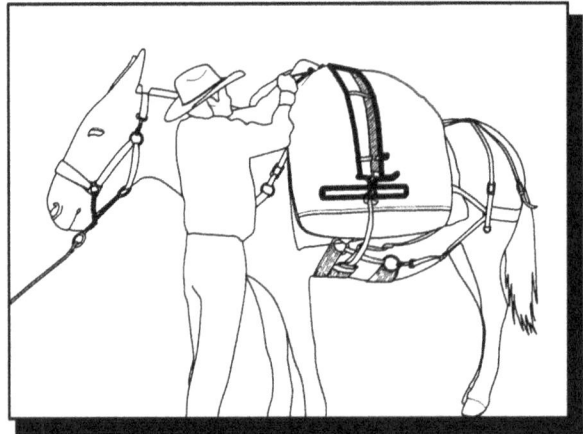

Figure 30–Securely tie each crosscut saw handle directly to the cinch ring or latigo, not to the load. Also tie the middle of the saw with a rope that attaches to the front sawbuck or the "D" ring of a Decker saddle.

Finish the packing job by using the cinch lash to tie the saw to the rest of the load (figure 31). That way, the saw is double-tied and unlikely to come loose.

Jim Thode of the Backcountry Horsemen of Washington has developed a rigid saw sheath that fits on a riding saddle (figure 32). This shoulder-to-rump sheath is loaded from the rear (figure 33). Fabrication details can be viewed on the Internet at *http://www.bchw.org/techtips.htm*. This sheath fits a 7-foot saw, unusually long for most trail work. A sheath sized for the more common $5\frac{1}{2}$-foot saw or single-person saw would be more useful. This type of sheath could be mounted under the load of a pack animal. It would be easy to slide the saw out alongside the animal from the rear to use to cut logs blocking the trail. Saws bowed and top-packed are difficult to unload and use enroute.

Figure 31–Finish the job by using the cinch lash to tie the saw to the rest of the load. This method is fine for moving a saw from home base to camp, but is very inconvenient if you need to use the saw along the trail.

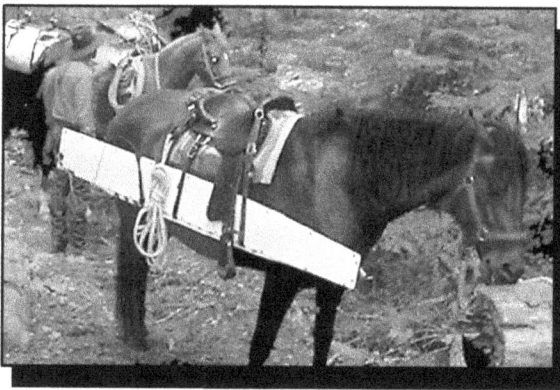

Figure 32–A rigid saw sheath configured for a riding saddle. This design also could be sized for a shorter saw, or used on a pack animal.—*Photo used with permission of Jim Thode, Lewis County Chapter of the Backcountry Horsemen of Washington.*

Figure 33—The sheath is made of $^3/_{16}$-inch high-density polyethylene, held together with countersunk copper rivets.—*Photo used with permission of Jim Thode, Lewis County Chapter of the Backcountry Horsemen of Washington.*

One-person saws can be transported on riding stock in a leather or canvas sheath (similar to a rifle scabbard). A piece of hardwood inside the sheath protects the sheath from the saw's teeth. Position the sheath so users will pull the saw away from the animal's head when they remove the saw from the sheath.

Hikers

Saws should be sheathed when you are hiking to the jobsite. The person carrying the saw should be the last person in line.

Two-person saws should have the rear handle removed. If the handle is left on, it can snag on branches. The handle's weight also accentuates the saw's bouncing motion.

At the jobsite, the unsheathed saw can be carried on your shoulder with the teeth facing outward (figure 34). Avoid carrying the saw with the teeth pointing inward. Carry the saw on your downhill shoulder so you can throw it off if you slip or fall.

Figure 34—Transporting a crosscut saw to a jobsite by carrying the saw on the shoulder with the teeth facing outward. Saws need to be sheathed when they are carried for long distances.

25

Longer two-person saws have a tendency to bounce severely on uneven trails. For this reason, I prefer a solid wood sheath. Wood is more rigid than firehose, so wooden sheaths have little bounce and are less tiring to carry.

A vintage saw can be bent around a pack if the saw is being carried for long distances. Usually both handles are left on the saw to secure it in its bent position. Do not bend the saw any more than necessary. In very rough or extremely brushy terrain I remove the handles, securing the ends of the saw with 12-gauge wire through the handle holes. This reduces the risk that the saw will hang up in brush.

Axes

The ax is a constant companion of the crosscut sawyer. It is not possible to be a proficient sawyer without mastering certain ax skills.

MTDC has published detailed information about axes that will not be repeated here. See Bernie Weisgerber's report, *An Ax to Grind: A Practical Ax Manual* (1999), and the accompanying two-part video, *An Ax to Grind* (1999). Another video, *Handtools for Trail Work, Parts 1 and 2* (1998) show ax and saw experts Ian Barlow and Dolly B. Chapman using crosscut saws and axes in the field.

Our brief coverage of axes will be limited to applications related to crosscut saws. These include using an ax while underbucking, driving wedges, and holding log segments in place while logs are being bucked. The ax is also recommended for cutting the undercut when trees are felled.

Safety Considerations

- Always remove branches, underbrush, overhead obstructions, or debris that might interfere with limbing and chopping.
- Do not allow anyone to stand in the immediate area.
- Make sure workers know how far materials may fly.
- Require that all workers wear the appropriate personal protective equipment.
- Always position your body securely while working with an ax.
- Never chop crosshanded; always use a natural striking action.
- Be alert when working on hillsides or uneven ground.
- If you cut a sapling that is held down by a fallen log (a spring pole), the sapling may spring back.
- If you have no need to cut something, leave it alone.
- Never use chopping tools as wedges or mauls.
- Do not allow two persons to chop or drive wedges together on the same tree.
- When chopping limbs from a felled tree, stand on the opposite side of the log from the limb being chopped and swing toward the top of the tree or branch.
- Do not allow the ax handle to drop below a plane parallel with the ground unless you are chopping on the side of a tree opposite your body.

Single-Bit Axes

Single-bit axes used for driving soft metal or plastic wedges need to be relatively heavy, usually 4 or 5 pounds. Driving aluminum or magnesium wedges will not harm an ax, but driving steel wedges with the poll (back of the head) of a single-bit ax may ruin it. Instead, carry a small single-jack hammer for driving steel wedges. Some sawyers carry only a single-bit ax with a straight handle and attempt to do everything with just one ax.

Wedges

The proper selection and use of wedges is of utmost importance when working with a crosscut saw. The crosscut sawyer depends on wedges more than the operator of a chain saw, but many crosscut sawyers do not have a good understanding of wedges or their uses.

The size, weight, and shape of wedges, and the material from which they are made vary with their intended use and the preferences of individual sawyers. I always take several wedges to cover ALL crosscut saw operations. I carry plastic and metal wedges in a couple of sizes. As a minimum, I carry a pair of hanging wedges and two plastic wedges.

Because the kerf made by a crosscut saw is often only one-fourth as wide as the kerf of a chain saw, the leading edge of crosscut wedges needs to have a sharper bevel than the leading edge of wedges used for chain saws. New plastic wedges should be filed to a thinner bevel before using. Wedges can be single, double, or triple tapered (figures 35 and 36).

Figure 35—A rifled single-taper wedge is designed to provide lift when a tree is felled. The wedge can be stacked with additional rifled single-taper wedges. The rifling helps keep the wedges aligned and stacked as they are being driven.

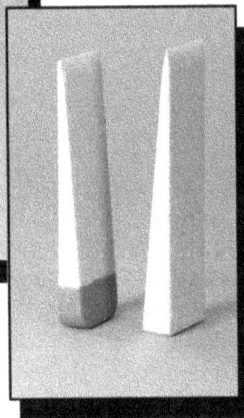

Figure 36—Double-taper wedges are designed to reduce bind.

Plastic wedges are good for felling operations. They do not split easily, and their textured surfaces provide additional holding power in the wood, helping to prevent the wedges from backing out when they are being driven. Plastic wedges are manufactured in a variety of sizes.

Although all wedges can be stacked (used one on top of the other), wedges may slip sideways if each wedge is not driven squarely. Newer wedge designs include "rifled" wedges. These wedges have a pair of grooves on one side and rails on the other. This design helps the wedges stay in place when they are stacked on each other.

Triple-taper wedges (figure 37) have a thin angle at the entry, an intermediate angle through most of the body, and a steeper angle near the top. I have not used many of these, but this design allows a shorter wedge to produce as much lift as a longer single-taper wedge. They are handy on small-diameter trees.

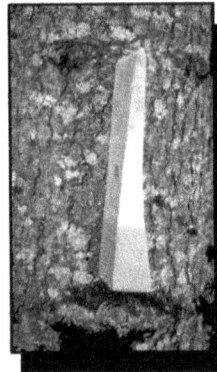

Figure 37—Triple-taper wedges allow a short wedge to provide as much lift as a longer wedge, but require more force to drive.

Always drive wedges by striking them squarely on the head. Drive them carefully to keep them from flying out of the cut.

Plastic wedges can break. If a long wedge can only be driven into the saw kerf a short way and refuses to go any farther, most of the wedge's length will be exposed, allowing a misplaced blow to break it. Use the shortest wedge possible that will accomplish your purpose. Hit the head squarely. Wedges should not be driven so tightly into the wood that blows deform the head of the wedge.

The sawyer should carry a single-bit ax or a single-jack hammer and an assortment of wedges. Plastic wedges occasionally get damaged, but they can be reshaped easily with a wood rasp or coarse file.

Wedges also are made of magnesium and aluminum. I like these soft metal wedges because they are so versatile (figure 38). They are light, stronger than plastic wedges, and

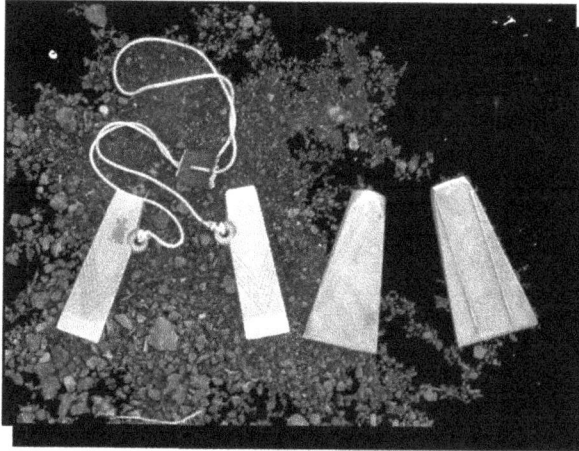

Figure 38—Wedges made from soft metals such as magnesium and aluminum are stronger than plastic, can be used as hanging wedges, and will not damage the saw.

Figure 39—Traditional metal wedges used for bucking and felling.

will not damage the saw. Unlike plastic wedges, they can be used as "tie wedges" or "hanging wedges" to keep a log from shifting as it is being bucked. Damaged soft metal wedges can be reshaped with a coarse metal file. Metal wedges can do the job of plastic wedges, but plastic wedges are no substitute for metal wedges.

Shallow grooves or depressions in the face of the wedge help prevent the wedge from backing out of cuts when the wedge is being driven. Wood fills the grooves and helps hold the wedge in place. Wedges with smooth faces can be roughened up with a cold chisel, helping achieve the same effect.

Felling Wedges

Felling wedges generally are longer and thinner than bucking or splitting wedges. Some felling wedges are only about 1 inch thick at the head and about 4 inches wide. Longer wedges—some as long as 13 inches—are available for large trees (figure 39).

Most felling wedges today are of the single-taper design and are made out of plastic or a soft metal, such as magnesium. Traditionally, wedges were made from durable wood or steel. Wooden wedges are not approved for crosscut saw use in the USDA Forest Service because they tend to split. For emergency use, wooden wedges can be fabricated in the field.

Felling wedges can be accurately described as lifting wedges. They are tapered on just one face and are truly an inclined plane. Metal and plastic single-taper wedges often have a groove on the flat sole face to increase holding power, while the inclined side is smooth to allow lifting.

Felling wedges exert force in the direction of the inclined plane. Two wedges can be stacked one on top of the other to produce more lift. Lifting wedges have many applications. They can be used to tighten, pry apart, or move materials. Exerting a force in one direction can be valuable. The sawyer may need to exert a force in one direction when getting a saw unstuck or when removing a chunk of log if the saw is bound.

When trees are being felled, single-taper wedges provide a way to lift the tree, preventing it from sitting back. A wedge must be inserted into the back cut as soon as possible. When logs are being bucked, wedges can reduce binds on the saw.

Bucking Wedges

Wedges used to reduce bind or split wood are double tapered, meaning that each of the broad faces tapers equally from the center. When such wedges are driven, wood moves away from both tapered sides equally.

Double-taper wedges are preferred for bucking, while single-taper wedges are used for felling. Both types of wedges keep the saw kerf from closing. However, the single-taper wedge used for felling performs a lifting function, while the double-taper wedge used for bucking pries the log apart. Crosscut saw bucking wedges are made of metal and are shorter than felling wedges. They are wider at the bottom and have more of a fan shape than a felling wedge (figure 40).

Bucking wedges traditionally were called *hanging wedges*, or sometimes *tie wedges*, on the West Coast. Hanging wedges got their name because sawyers carried a lanyard, or cord, with a pair of wedges around their neck. The wedges are used as a pair, one driven across the kerf at the 10 o'clock position and the other driven across the kerf at the 2 o'clock position. Buckers usually sunk their ax on the uphill or least movable log segment tightly above the cord so when the log segments came free, the wedges would not fall onto the saw. I recommend that every crosscut sawyer have a pair of these metal bucking wedges.

Figure 40—A bucking wedge being used as a hanging wedge. The wedge kept the cut from opening too quickly and splitting the log, and also stopped the log from rolling on the bucker when the cut was finished.—Now You're Logging. *by Bus Griffiths, with permission of Harbour Publishing, Madeira Park, BC, Canada*

Underbucks

Underbucks help hold the saw in position when the saw is cutting from underneath the log. They also act as a fulcrum. A good sawyer can cut as fast—or faster—from underneath a log as from the top. When the sawyer applies a downward pressure on the handle, the saw is forced up into the log.

Axes for Underbucking

Axes are often used to support the saw when underbucking. Axes used for underbucking typically have a straight, but slightly modified 36-inch wooden handle.

You can modify an ax for underbucking by cutting two series of three notches on one side of the handle about 6 inches from the end (figure 41). The grooves are far enough away from your gripping hand that they won't affect you when you chop with the ax. The series of three notches, placed about an inch apart, will allow you to line up one of the notches with the cut. The notches should be 30 to 45 degrees off perpendicular to allow room for the saw between the ax handle and the log. The shallow notches should not be cut into the grip portion of the handle.

Because it has a symmetrical handle, a double-bit ax is often the tool of choice for underbucking. Some less-experienced sawyers like to use a single-bit ax as an underbuck because they can drive the head with a single-jack hammer to better position the ax handle. I prefer the double-bit ax because of the versatility of having two blades.

Often a sawyer will dedicate a less-than-favorite ax to underbucking by flat grinding the cheeks of the ax head to a wedge shape. This shape allows more of the head to stick firmly into the log. This is great for underbucking, but ruins the ax for chopping because the blade sticks on every chop. However, if one blade of a double-bit ax is modified in this way, the other blade will remain usable for chopping.

Mechanical Underbucks

Sometimes mechanical underbucks (figure 42) are used instead of an ax. Some underbucks attach to an ax, others are sheaves that fit over an ax handle, and still others are

Figure 41—A double-bit ax that has been modified and grooved for underbucking. Usually a less-than-favorite ax was dedicated to this purpose.—Now You're Logging, by Bus Griffiths, with permission of Harbour Publishing, Madeira Park, BC, Canada

Figure 42—This vintage mechanical underbuck helps hold the saw up so it can cut from beneath the log. This is one design of many that were available.

stand-alone tools. Most underbucks have a groove or roller on the end to serve as a guide for the back of the saw. This groove or roller needs to be adjusted properly to align the saw cut.

Vintage underbucks are hard to find. Homemade underbucks are easy to make out of a small leaf spring, a clamp, and a pulley. Custom underbucks also are available.

Mechanical underbucks are thought to increase production because they reduce friction as the saw traveled over the ax handle. But many buckers do not use them because they do not want to pack heavy tools through the woods.

I have a small vintage underbuck that clamps onto the ax handle. It allows the saw back to run in a sheave groove. I believe this lightweight underbuck, coupled with a modified, thinner ax head, is the best solution for much of our trail work.

A MTDC report by Chuck Whitlock, *Crosscut Saw Underbucking Tool* (2002), shows how to fabricate a similar lightweight underbucking tool (figure 43). This new model is not as good as my vintage underbuck. It would benefit by having a larger bearing surface on the ax, and a different clamp tightener that does not interfere with the saw at certain angles.

Figure 43—The MTDC underbuck features a 2-inch clamp with a shielded steel pulley. It attaches to an ax handle.

Lubricants

Lubricant is probably a misnomer in crosscut saw terminology, but it persists. Saw teeth do not need to be lubricated as they cut. The friction of the saw tooth set against the kerf keeps the teeth reasonably clean. Resin deposits on the lower part of the teeth and in the saw gullets do produce drag. Lubricants soften these deposits and help remove them. The lubricant serves more as a solvent than as a lubricating agent.

Cutting in extremely wet environments or during a hard rain can cause wood fibers to swell. In these conditions, a lubricant can help reduce drag.

Traditionally, crosscut saw lubricants were petroleum based. Diesel fuel and kerosene were the most common lubricants and were effective. Because of environmental concerns and the possible health hazards of petroleum-based solvents, the USDA Forest Service now recommends citrus or water-based solvents. Some tree resins can be removed with water.

Applying Lubricants

Squeeze bottles allow the sawyer or a helper to direct a stream of lubricant onto the saw's surfaces. On the push stroke, the sawyer keeps one hand on the saw handle and uses the other hand to apply the lubricant to one side of the saw blade. The sawyer lubricates the other side of the blade on the next push stroke.

Aerosol cans or spray bottles do not deliver enough lubricant to the saw blade to be successful. However, after the saw has been cleaned with a solvent at the end of the day, a thin coating of light oil can be applied with an aerosol can or spray bottle.

Old photos show crosscut sawyers using a corked whiskey bottle or Japanese sake bottle to hold their lubricants. I still like this method because it is simple and efficient (figure 44).

Figure 44—A traditional oil bottle applies liberal amounts of saw lubricant. The hook held the bottle to the log, conveniently within reach.—Now You're Logging, *by Bus Griffiths, with permission of Harbour Publishing, Madeira Park, BC, Canada*

To make a corked bottle, select a round bottle, about a quart in size, with a screw cap. Bottles need to be thick, with a neck that is easy to grab. Lash a sharp hook (that will stick in the tree or log) to the bottle's neck and insert a slotted cork or rubber stopper into the bottle's mouth. Rubber is easier to work. Two bottles, one for each sawyer, are convenient when bucking large logs. The slotted cork is used to protect the hook point, an important safety consideration, when the bottle's cap is screwed on for transport.

Experiment with the length, number, and size of the slots in the cork or rubber stopper. I usually cut three grooves in the cork, depending on the width and depth of each groove. You shake the liquid out instead of pouring it.

Some sawyers use a plastic squeeze bottle with a slotted cork. They remove the solid cap at the jobsite and insert the cork. The liquid is applied by simultaneously shaking and squeezing the bottle. Make sure the cork is tight so it won't pop off under pressure.

Instead of a slotted cork, sawyers in the past stuffed pine needles or grass into the top of the bottle to control the flow.

Preparation for Bucking and Felling

Safety Considerations

Great care needs to be taken when bucking or felling. The same principles apply whether a crosscut saw or a chain saw is used, but the sawyer is exposed to risks longer during crosscut saw operations. However, the crosscut sawyer can better bear the forces acting on the wood than a chain saw operator.

Never attempt any action that you cannot handle or if you are unsure of the prob-able outcome. Always be ready to adjust your cutting strategy based on how forces are affecting the cut.

Personal Protective Equipment

Less personal protective equipment is required to use a crosscut saw than is required to operate a chain saw. Although chaps and ear protection are needed to operate a chain saw, they generally are not required to use a crosscut saw.

Crosscut sawyers require eye protection because chips can fly when chopping or wedging and the wind can blow shavings into their eyes. Hardhats, work boots, appropriate gloves, long-sleeved shirts, and long pants also are required. Soft hats, tennis shoes, T-shirts, and shorts are not acceptable.

You should wear leather or cut-resistant fabric gloves. Handling a hot saw left in the sun, placing and removing sheaths, and other hazardous activities all require gloves. Cotton gloves are not acceptable. Wear proper-fitting gloves when sawing.

Boots are required when using a crosscut saw. Boots are defined in the USDA Forest Service's *Health and Safety Code Handbook* (FSH 6709.11) as: *Heavy-duty, cut resistant or leather, waterproof or water-repellent, 8-inch high laced boots with nonskid soles (hard toes are optional).*

A first aid kit must be available at the worksite. Other safety considerations such as a medical evacuation plan, provisions for radio use, and local policies (such as restrictions on working alone) must be followed by crosscut sawyers and need to be documented in the job hazard analysis (JHA).

Determining the Forces on the Log

When cutting a log, three main forces need to be considered: wood under compression, wood under tension, and gravity (figure 45).

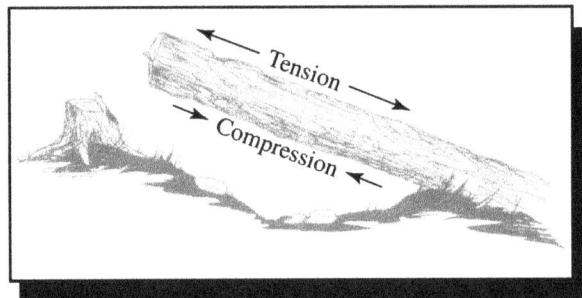

Figure 45—The log is being pulled apart by tension force and pushed together by compression force. Areas of tension and compression occur on opposite sides of the log.

Wood under compression wants to push together when it is severed. Compression wood causes crosscut saws to bind. Chain saws often can cut out minor compression, but crosscut saws cannot. Compression wood will completely bind the saw. Using wedges properly is more critical with crosscut saws than with chain saws. Crosscut sawyers should develop wedging skills to a high level.

Wood under tension wants to separate when it is severed. Tension, especially when combined with gravity, can be very powerful. Whenever wood is under tension in one part of a log, wood will be under compression somewhere else.

Understanding gravity helps the sawyer to work safely. Unlike the forces of tension and compression, the force of gravity is constant.

Situational Awareness

Plan the bucking cut carefully after considering:

- The escape route
- Slope
- Tension
- Compression
- Rocks and foreign objects on the log
- Pivot points
- Adequate saw clearance
- Overhead hazards
- The limits of your ability
- The length of the saw in relation to the log being bucked
- People and property in the cutting zone
- Spring poles
- Proper tool placement
- Falling or rolling root wads
- The log's tendency to roll, slide, or bind
- Broken-off limbs underneath the log that can hook the sawyer if the log rolls
- Safe footing

Bucking Sizeup

Sizing up the bucking situation means that the sawyer must visualize the hazards and consequences of each cutting action. This step is very important.

Overhead Hazards

Visually scan all adjacent trees. A fallen tree blocking the trail may have left broken limbs hanging in adjacent trees as it fell. These hanging limbs or trees are called widow makers.. They can become dislodged and fall at any time.

Do not work beneath any hazard that could come down on you or cause a chain reaction that may strike you. Winds can be a legitimate reason to suspend bucking when hazards are overhead.

Side Slopes

Assess the position of a fallen tree in relation to the slope. If the log lies straight up and down the fall line, end bind will be a concern. The safe uphill side of the log is easy to identify if the log lies parallel to the slope. If the

log lies at a different angle, the safe uphill side will not be so easy to identify. Slope, pivot points, gravity, soil hardness and other factors all need to be considered.

Having good footing is extremely important. Take time to kick out a solid footing before beginning to buck.

On steep slopes it's sometimes a good idea to put a block of wood under the downhill side of the log to prevent it from rolling. The log may damage the saw and the trail if it rolls. The block of wood should be about a foot long with a sound limb on it. Remove the bark on the block to reduce friction and leave the limb up so you can pull the block out later.

When the log is severed, the wedges should allow it to settle against the block. While standing in a safe location, remove the wedges and use the limb to wiggle the block out. Never finish a cut on the downhill side of a log.

Spring Poles

Spring poles (figure 46) are limbs or saplings that are bent beneath a fallen tree. A spring pole can store a tremendous amount of energy. Spring poles can be dangerous if they are cut accidentally, or without careful planning. Cut a spring pole only when necessary.

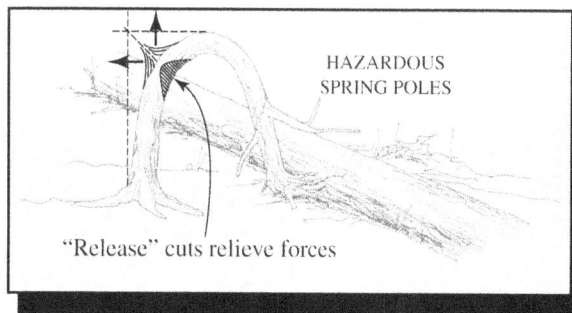

Figure 46—Look out for spring poles (trees or limbs that are being held down by other trees). Spring poles can release with great force, causing serious injuries. Make a series of small cuts on the inside of the bend when severing a spring pole.

Before cutting a spring pole, select the best spot to make the cut. One way to do so is to determine a point where two projected lines intersect. The first line extends vertically from the base of the spring pole. The second line projects horizontally from the extreme top of the pole's bend. From the intersection of these lines, a 45-degree angle projected back to the spring pole marks the preferred place to make a series of release cuts. This technique is also used when determining where to cut bent limbs. In those cases, *horizontal* and *vertical* become relative terms.

If other safety factors do not prevent you from severing the spring pole at the calculated spot, make a series of small cuts on the side under compression. This is always the inside of the bend. Your cutting position and escape routes need to be carefully considered. You must understand the direction the cut ends will travel when planning a safe escape route.

Never use two sawyers when cutting spring poles.

Do not use a crosscut saw to release a spring pole unless the pole is very large. If a crosscut saw is used, a one-person saw with smaller teeth on the front is preferred. Regular crosscut saw tooth patterns usually do not allow the carefully controlled cuts needed to release spring poles.

Some sawyers prefer to use the small teeth on the extreme end of a crosscut saw because the teeth are finer and because doing so provides more distance from the cut material. My experience has taught me that being closer and in absolute control of my carefully placed cuts is safer than being farther back.

I prefer to use the small folding pruning saw that I carry in my day pack. It provides me the most control over the amount of wood fiber being severed. I do not use a crosscut saw for cutting spring poles except in rare situations, usually associated with limbing, where physical barriers prevent me from using the small saw. An ax or Pulaski also may be used, but be careful to limit the depth of each cut. Releasing compression with an ax requires light hacking or nicking rather than actual chopping.

When using a saw, I cut into the compression wood until the sapling moves or the saw starts to bind. I cut no farther and remove the saw quickly. I place an identical cut about one to one-and-one-half times the sapling's diameter away. When this cut binds, I remove the saw and place a third cut between the first two cuts but closer to the first cut than the second. Usually I can cut a little deeper than I did with the first cut. I continue alternating back and forth, working toward the center between these cuts, always vigilant for the

tension side to rip apart and the spring pole ends to fly away from me. By the time I have made a number of cuts, some of the energy stored in the wood fibers has been removed, making the final break less violent.

The most common form of spring poles encountered by crosscut sawyers during trail clearing are the limbs on the underside of a green tree that has fallen across a trail. If the spring poles are directly under the tree, the limb usually strikes the dirt directly beneath it when the limb is severed. The more hazardous limbs are those located along the sides of the log. These limbs can fly outward when severed.

Avoid making the common mistake of severing bent limbs at the bole of the tree. Always cut at the spot indicated by the intersection of the projected lines, even if it means making a second cut flush with the bole later so the log can be rolled off the trail. Cutting limbs under great pressure at the bole of the tree rather than at the spot indicated by the intersection of the projected lines exposes the sawyer to much greater risk. Be especially careful to clean out a safe working area before cutting these spring pole limbs. I save them for last, after I have removed all other vegetation and have secured a safe working area with escape routes.

Suspended Logs

Cutting a suspended log is a single-buck (one person) operation. Often only one side is safe or has adequate footing for you to make the cut.

If you are standing on blowdown where several trees are jackstrawed in different directions, carefully evaluate the sequence in which trees should be removed. Resist the temptation to dive in and cut the first log you come across. Generally, the bottom logs should be cut and removed first. This practice reduces the chance that logs or other material on top will move.

Be sure there is a safe path for any cut log to follow. This is the reason I remove the bottom logs first. If you cut from the top down, the top logs can fall between bottom logs, making the bottom logs impossible to cut.

Proper use of skid logs makes dealing with jackstrawed blowdown safer and easier. Skid logs are placed underneath the log you are cutting to make it easier to move. Calculate the results of your planned sequence of cuts, so that you will have skid logs properly positioned to help move the log where you want it to go. Sometimes those logs support the log as it is being cut.

It might not be possible to remove all suspended trees with a saw. Take out only the ones that can be removed safely. Other suspended trees could be removed with winches or explosives, if necessary.

Often, suspended logs roll when they are released. Be sure the log has a safe path to travel. Logs may ricochet off other objects, making their paths unpredictable. Be sure no snags or other weak trees are in the log's path. They could snap if the log strikes them. Fell snags or weak trees first, if they can be felled safely.

Pivot Points

Pivot points are high points on the ground, or a rock, stump, log, or even limbs on the lower side of a log, that catch part of a moving log and cause it to pivot unexpectedly. Pivot points can be very dangerous and may not be easy to detect. The pivot point acts as a lever in either the vertical or horizontal plane. A log lying on an undetected rock can shift violently upward when the log is bucked. A rolling log caught at its midpoint can swing back uphill or sideways toward the unsuspecting sawyer.

Side Binds

Side binds occur when one side of the log is under compression and the other is under tension. Side bind usually occurs when a log has fallen and is resting between a couple of trees or other obstructions. Cut the compression side first and finish by cutting the side under tension. This cut can be difficult, because it may require sawing from a vertical position. Instead of sawing out side binds, I usually chop them out if they are not too large. Chopping is safer.

Rootwad Movement

Take a close look at logs still attached to their upended rootwads. Are the rootwads going to move when they are severed from the rest of the tree? Where will they move? If the tree is green or the ground is very wet, the roots may be bent over and under a lot of pressure. Try to dig under the rootwad to evaluate any major roots you may not see. These are similar to spring poles, but are more difficult to detect. Spring pole roots also may act as pivot points, causing the tree to swing when the bole is severed.

Rootwads that have no firm attachment to the ground can roll easily, especially on steep slopes, or if the bole is severed near the rootwad. I sometimes secure rootwads by attaching a winch cable to them so I can apply direct holding pressure. This technique also helps to reduce end bind. A rope works just as well. The idea is to keep the rootwad in place.

Unsound Wood

Rotten wood can crack or break without warning. Logs may be sound in one part and rotten in another. Examine the ends of logs and look for indications of rot. Observe the color of shavings the saw is producing. Dark shavings indicate rot. Rotten wood doesn't hold wedges well, making them ineffective. Because rotten logs may hold more moisture, saws tend to load up with shavings, increasing the need for wedges to keep the kerf open.

Test for soundness by thumping the log with the poll of a single-bit ax. The ax will rebound from the sound wood and the thump will produce a high-pitch noise. Rotten wood has a hollow, low-pitch sound. Loose bark can be a problem to the crosscut saw bucker, although loose bark is not as hazardous on a fallen tree as on a standing tree. Remove loose bark before bucking. Vertical or spiral cracks may indicate weakness and can cause a log to spiral open, especially when it is bucked on steep side hills. Fire-weakened trees need to be sized up carefully as well.

Log Movement

Assume that most logs will move when bucked. Not all log movement is hazardous, but even the slightest movement can pinch a crosscut saw, bend it, or damage the saw's set. Larger logs present more potential risk because their center of gravity is higher and they are heavier.

the results of your planned sequence of cuts, so that you will have skid logs properly positioned to help move the log where you want it to go. Sometimes those logs support the log as it is being cut.

It might not be possible to remove all suspended trees with a saw. Take out only the ones that can be removed safely. Other suspended trees could be removed with winches or explosives, if necessary.

Often, suspended logs roll when they are released. Be sure the log has a safe path to travel. Logs may ricochet off other objects, making their paths unpredictable. Be sure no snags or other weak trees are in the log's path. They could snap if the log strikes them. Fell snags or weak trees first, if they can be felled safely.

Pivot Points

Pivot points are high points on the ground, or a rock, stump, log, or even limbs on the lower side of a log, that catch part of a moving log and cause it to pivot unexpectedly. Pivot points can be very dangerous and may not be easy to detect. The pivot point acts as a lever in either the vertical or horizontal plane. A log lying on an undetected rock can shift violently upward when the log is bucked. A rolling log caught at its midpoint can swing back uphill or sideways toward the unsuspecting sawyer.

Side Binds

Side binds occur when one side of the log is under compression and the other is under tension. Side bind usually occurs when a log has fallen and is resting between a couple of trees or other obstructions. Cut the compression side first and finish by cutting the side under tension. This cut can be difficult, because it may require sawing from a vertical position. Instead of sawing out side binds, I usually chop them out if they are not too large. Chopping is safer.

Rootwad Movement

Take a close look at logs still attached to their upended rootwads. Are the rootwads going to move when they are severed from the rest of the tree? Where will they move? If the tree is green or the ground is very wet, the roots may be bent over and under a lot of pressure. Try to dig under the rootwad to evaluate any major roots you may not see. These are similar to spring poles, but are more difficult to detect. Spring pole roots also may act as pivot points, causing the tree to swing when the bole is severed.

Rootwads that have no firm attachment to the ground can roll easily, especially on steep slopes, or if the bole is severed near the rootwad. I sometimes secure rootwads by attaching a winch cable to them so I can apply direct holding pressure. This technique also helps to reduce end bind. A rope works just as well. The idea is to keep the rootwad in place.

Unsound Wood

Rotten wood can crack or break without warning. Logs may be sound in one part and rotten in another. Examine the ends of logs and look for indications of rot. Observe the color of shavings the saw is producing. Dark shavings indicate rot. Rotten wood doesn't hold wedges well, making them ineffective. Because rotten logs may hold more moisture, saws tend to load up with shavings, increasing the need for wedges to keep the kerf open.

Test for soundness by thumping the log with the poll of a single-bit ax. The ax will rebound from the sound wood and the thump will produce a high-pitch noise. Rotten wood has a hollow, low-pitch sound. Loose bark can be a problem to the crosscut saw bucker, although loose bark is not as hazardous on a fallen tree as on a standing tree. Remove loose bark before bucking. Vertical or spiral cracks may indicate weakness and can cause a log to spiral open, especially when it is bucked on steep side hills. Fire-weakened trees need to be sized up carefully as well.

Log Movement

Assume that most logs will move when bucked. Not all log movement is hazardous, but even the slightest movement can pinch a crosscut saw, bend it, or damage the saw's set. Larger logs present more potential risk because their center of gravity is higher and they are heavier.

Planning the Cut

Think the cut through. Make sure that you have the correct saw, the right complement of wedges, and an ax or single-jack hammer to drive them. Know exactly where each cut will go, the types of cuts you will need, and the sequence of the cuts.

Figure out what the severed log is likely to do, and what you would like it to do. You can sometimes control the log by managing the energy that is released when the log is severed. You can retard energy release with wedges or with blocks that prevent the log from rolling. You can accelerate energy release by using ramped skid logs. Expert crosscut saw users apply the principles of force and movement to get the log to its final resting place.

Can the log be bucked safely with existing skills and equipment? Sawyers should not feel pressured to perform any task that is beyond their ability. Ask other crewmembers to size up the situation silently. Discuss your findings afterward. Listen to dissenters. Sizeups based on "group think" where dissenters' views are not expressed or not considered often miss important factors.

Shattered logs are especially troublesome, because each splintered section may have its own bind. The sawyer may have to cut first from one side, then move to the other. Chopping out a V-notch with an ax is another good alternative to cutting it with a saw.

Types of Cuts

The three basic types of cuts are: the straight, compound, and offset. Each type of cut and its usual application (figure 47) is described.

A straight cut is made through the log, usually starting from the top. It can be performed by single or double bucking.

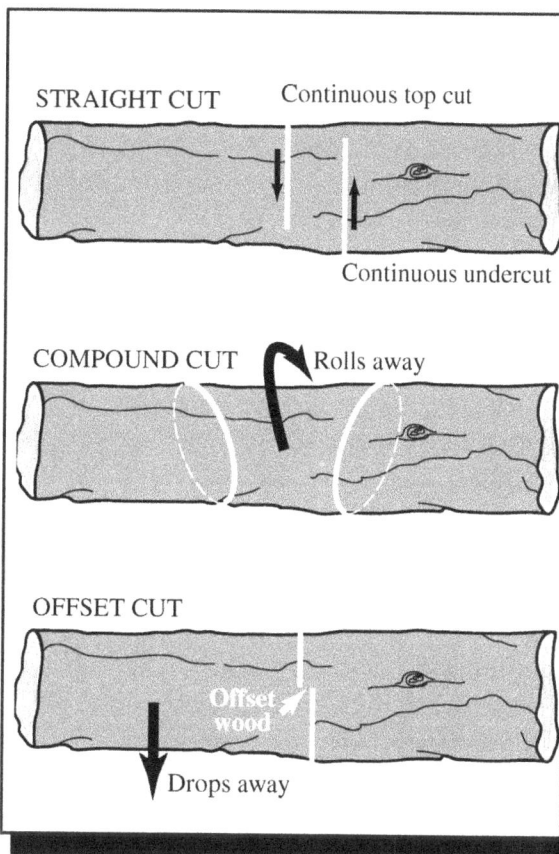

Figure 47—Three basic cuts: straight, compound, and offset.

It can also be cut continuously from underneath the log by a single sawyer using an underbuck.

The forces on the log allow the saw to cut through the log only with the help of wedges. Unfortunately, inexperienced buckers sometimes try to use a straight cut when a compound or offset cut is needed. When a saw is bound tight in a log, the bucker probably used a straight cut inappropriately.

A compound cut is placed at an angle that is narrower than perpendicular to the log and angled so that the bottom of the cut slopes toward the part of the log that is being removed. This cut typically is used when clearing a large log that is across a trail. Two cuts need to be made and the severed chunk of the log has to be removed.

By placing a compound cut so that the severed log is longer on the downhill side, the bottom of the cut log is

Planning the Cut

Think the cut through. Make sure that you have the correct saw, the right complement of wedges, and an ax or single-jack hammer to drive them. Know exactly where each cut will go, the types of cuts you will need, and the sequence of the cuts.

Figure out what the severed log is likely to do, and what you would like it to do. You can sometimes control the log by managing the energy that is released when the log is severed. You can retard energy release with wedges or with blocks that prevent the log from rolling. You can accelerate energy release by using ramped skid logs. Expert crosscut saw users apply the principles of force and movement to get the log to its final resting place.

Can the log be bucked safely with existing skills and equipment? Sawyers should not feel pressured to perform any task that is beyond their ability. Ask other crewmembers to size up the situation silently. Discuss your findings afterward. Listen to dissenters. Sizeups based on "group think" where dissenters' views are not expressed or not considered often miss important factors.

Shattered logs are especially troublesome, because each splintered section may have its own bind. The sawyer may have to cut first from one side, then move to the other. Chopping out a V-notch with an ax is another good alternative to cutting it with a saw.

Types of Cuts

The three basic types of cuts are: the straight, compound, and offset. Each type of cut and its usual application (figure 47) is described.

A straight cut is made through the log, usually starting from the top. It can be performed by single or double bucking.

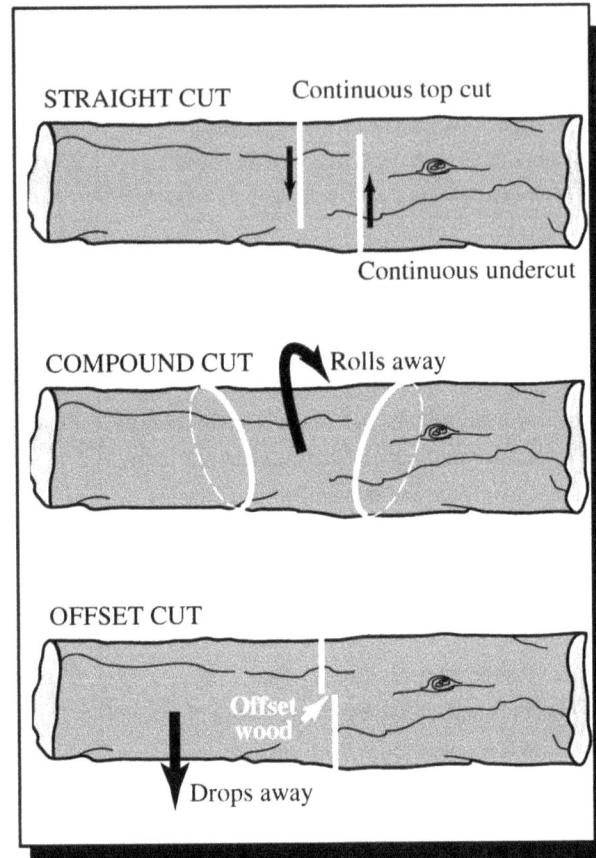

Figure 47—Three basic cuts: straight, compound, and offset.

It can also be cut continuously from underneath the log by a single sawyer using an underbuck.

The forces on the log allow the saw to cut through the log only with the help of wedges. Unfortunately, inexperienced buckers sometimes try to use a straight cut when a compound or offset cut is needed. When a saw is bound tight in a log, the bucker probably used a straight cut inappropriately.

A compound cut is placed at an angle that is narrower than perpendicular to the log and angled so that the bottom of the cut slopes toward the part of the log that is being removed. This cut typically is used when clearing a large log that is across a trail. Two cuts need to be made and the severed chunk of the log has to be removed.

By placing a compound cut so that the severed log is longer on the downhill side, the bottom of the cut log is narrower than the top of the cut log. This reduces the chance that the log will bind when it is rolled out of the way. This cut is performed either as a straight cut or as a combination of top cut and undercut.

The offset cut is placed so that the bottom underbucking cut *does not* match up exactly with the top cut.

This kind of underbucking operation is used when a log is suspended and will drop free when severed. Once the top cut has been made, a single sawyer selects a groove (about $\frac{1}{2}$ inch toward the ax head from the top kerf) from the grooves cut into the saw handle or installs a mechanical underbuck. The ax head is always secured to the side of the log that won't move when the log is cut.

In underbucking, offset wood prevents the severed log from damaging the saw or causing injury when the log drops. This small amount of offset wood acts like the holding wood left when trees are felled. In felling, the holding wood keeps the tree from kicking back.

Determining the Safe Working Side of the Log

Whether you are sawing alone or in tandem, you need to determine the safe working side of the log. This is the side where the final cut will be made.

Planning and Clearing Escape Routes

Escape routes when bucking need to be thought of differently than escape routes when felling, but the principle is the same. Determine danger zones and plan an escape route that avoids them. Clear debris along the route. Although you may not have to use your escape route, your life may depend on it if a log pivots or another problem arises.

Establishing a Work Platform

Because crosscut sawing requires good balance, you need a fairly level platform under your feet. Remove logs, branches, brush, and other vegetation. Use a digging tool to create footholds on steep ground.

Saw blades work best when they are operated perpendicular to the force of gravity. Keeping saws level often requires cutting from a kneeling or crouching position. Kneeling or half-kneeling is better than crouching, both for ergonomic reasons and to maintain control over the cut. Too often a sawyer working from a crouch allows the saw to hit the dirt on the offside of the log, or the saw pinches because the sawyer left too much holding wood on the near side of the log.

Providing Adequate Saw Clearance

Remove rocks and dirt under the log that could dull the saw. I try to dig under the log and place bark or other soft material there to protect the saw when it finishes the cut. Remove all vegetation from the path of the saw.

Bark Removal

The bark on logs often contains sand, dirt, and small rocks that can dull the saw. Fire-charred logs also dull saws. Most crosscut sawyers remove the bark with an ax before starting to cut. In addition, bark is spongy and can reduce the effectiveness of wedges. Remove enough of the bark so that wedges will contact firm wood.

Tool Placement

I usually place wedges and axes on top of a large log where either the uphill or downhill sawyer can reach them. Do not place tools on top of the log if they can fall on the downhill sawyer. The sawyer at the uphill position will set the top- and near-side wedges and ensure the safety of the lower sawyer. The lower sawyer sets the hanging wedge on his or her side of the log, if it is needed.

I often place skids under the log so it won't drop into a hole or trench. Long steel rock bars work as skids; so do native poles. Leave branch stubs about 2 to 3 inches long on the bottom of the skid to help anchor it. If extremely heavy log segments need to be skidded, I use a green tree with the bark removed for a skid. I can make the peeled log slide more easily by pouring water on it.

Crew Communication

Clear communication among all crew members is vital for safety and efficiency. Be sure everyone knows the planned sequence of events. Know where the severed log is going to narrower than the top of the cut log. This reduces the chance that the log will bind when it is rolled out of the way. This cut is performed either as a straight cut or as a combination of top cut and undercut.

The offset cut is placed so that the bottom underbucking cut *does not* match up exactly with the top cut.

This kind of underbucking operation is used when a log is suspended and will drop free when severed. Once the top cut has been made, a single sawyer selects a groove (about $1/2$ inch toward the ax head from the top kerf) from the grooves cut into the saw handle or installs a mechanical underbuck. The ax head is always secured to the side of the log that won't move when the log is cut.

In underbucking, offset wood prevents the severed log from damaging the saw or causing injury when the log drops. This small amount of offset wood acts like the holding wood left when trees are felled. In felling, the holding wood keeps the tree from kicking back.

Determining the Safe Working Side of the Log

Whether you are sawing alone or in tandem, you need to determine the safe working side of the log. This is the side where the final cut will be made.

Planning and Clearing Escape Routes

Escape routes when bucking need to be thought of differently than escape routes when felling, but the principle is the same. Determine danger zones and plan an escape route that avoids them. Clear debris along the route. Although you may not have to use your escape route, your life may depend on it if a log pivots or another problem arises.

Establishing a Work Platform

Because crosscut sawing requires good balance, you need a fairly level platform under your feet. Remove logs, branches, brush, and other vegetation. Use a digging tool to create footholds on steep ground.

Saw blades work best when they are operated perpendicular to the force of gravity. Keeping saws level often requires cutting from a kneeling or crouching position. Kneeling or half-kneeling is better than crouching, both for

ergonomic reasons and to maintain control over the cut. Too often a sawyer working from a crouch allows the saw to hit the dirt on the offside of the log, or the saw pinches because the sawyer left too much holding wood on the near side of the log.

Providing Adequate Saw Clearance

Remove rocks and dirt under the log that could dull the saw. I try to dig under the log and place bark or other soft material there to protect the saw when it finishes the cut. Remove all vegetation from the path of the saw.

Bark Removal

The bark on logs often contains sand, dirt, and small rocks that can dull the saw. Fire-charred logs also dull saws. Most crosscut sawyers remove the bark with an ax before starting to cut. In addition, bark is spongy and can reduce the effectiveness of wedges. Remove enough of the bark so that wedges will contact firm wood.

Tool Placement

I usually place wedges and axes on top of a large log where either the uphill or downhill sawyer can reach them. Do not place tools on top of the log if they can fall on the downhill sawyer. The sawyer at the uphill position will set the top- and near-side wedges and ensure the safety of the lower sawyer. The lower sawyer sets the hanging wedge on his or her side of the log, if it is needed.

I often place skids under the log so it won't drop into a hole or trench. Long steel rock bars work as skids; so do native poles. Leave branch stubs about 2 to 3 inches long on the bottom of the skid to help anchor it. If extremely heavy log segments need to be skidded, I use a green tree with the bark removed for a skid. I can make the peeled log slide more easily by pouring water on it.

Crew Communication

Clear communication among all crew members is vital for safety and efficiency. Be sure everyone knows the planned sequence of events. Know where the severed log is going to roll. If a portion of the trail is below the path of the log, post a trail guard in a safe place to warn unsuspecting visitors of the hazard. Be sure everyone knows who will give the *all clear* signal.

Determining Binds

Understanding directional forces, or binds, is important. Binds determine bucking techniques and procedures.

Landforms, stumps, blowdown, and other obstacles that prevent a log from lying flat cause binds. The four types of bind are: top, bottom, side, and end (figure 48). It is possible for logs to have no bind. Normally, logs have a combination of two or more binds:

- **Top Bind**—The tension is on the bottom of the log. The compression is on the top.
- **Bottom Bind**—The tension is on the top of the log. The compression is on the bottom.
- **Side Bind**—Pressure is exerted sideways on the log.
- **End Bind**—Weight compresses the log's entire cross section.
- **No Bind**—This log could be cut without a wedge and it would not move. It is difficult to predict binds, so a safe practice is to wedge logs even though you don't think they have binds.

Determining Bucking Locations

It is best to start bucking at the top of the log and work toward the butt end, removing the binds in smaller material first. Bucking is generally a single-person operation. Two sawyers may be used when it is safe to do so.

Determine the offside (figure 49). The offside is the side the log will probably move to when it is cut, normally the downhill side. Watch out for possible pivots. Clear the work area and escape route. The work area should be at least 8 feet wide in the vicinity of the log to allow plenty of room for escape when the final cut is made. Establish solid footing and remove any debris that may hinder your escape.

Cut the offside first. If possible, make a cut about one-third the diameter of the log. This allows the sawyer to step back from the log on the final cut.

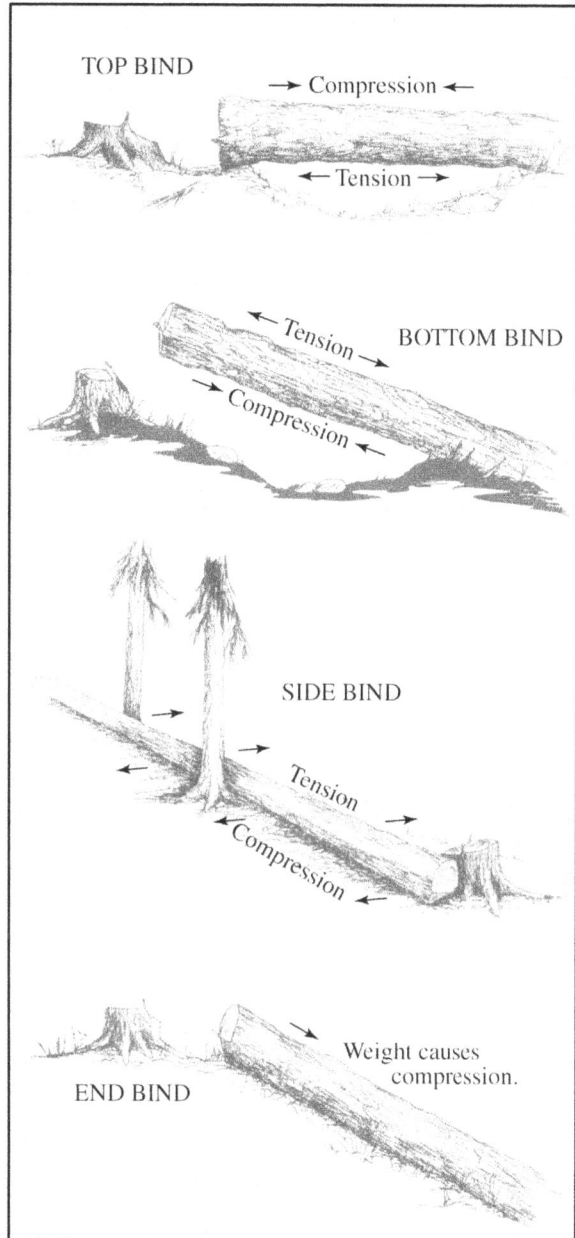

Figure 48—There are four types of binds. A log can have a combination of two or more binds.

Points to Remember When Planning the Cut

- Do a complete sizeup. Identify the hazards and establish your escape routes and safety zones.
- Use objects such as rocks, stumps (if they are tall enough), and sound standing trees (with no overhead hazards) to

40

roll. If a portion of the trail is below the path of the log, post a trail guard in a safe place to warn unsuspecting visitors of the hazard. Be sure everyone knows who will give the *all clear* signal.

Determining Binds

Understanding directional forces, or binds, is important. Binds determine bucking techniques and procedures.

Landforms, stumps, blowdown, and other obstacles that prevent a log from lying flat cause binds. The four types of bind are: top, bottom, side, and end (figure 48). It is possible for logs to have no bind. Normally, logs have a combination of two or more binds:

- **Top Bind**—The tension is on the bottom of the log. The compression is on the top.
- **Bottom Bind**—The tension is on the top of the log. The compression is on the bottom.
- **Side Bind**—Pressure is exerted sideways on the log.
- **End Bind**—Weight compresses the log's entire cross section.
- **No Bind**—This log could be cut without a wedge and it would not move. It is difficult to predict binds, so a safe practice is to wedge logs even though you don't think they have binds.

Determining Bucking Locations

It is best to start bucking at the top of the log and work toward the butt end, removing the binds in smaller material first. Bucking is generally a single-person operation. Two sawyers may be used when it is safe to do so.

Determine the offside (figure 49). The offside is the side the log will probably move to when it is cut, normally the downhill side. Watch out for possible pivots. Clear the work area and escape route. The work area should be at least 8 feet wide in the vicinity of the log to allow plenty of room for escape when the final cut is made. Establish solid footing and remove any debris that may hinder your escape.

Cut the offside first. If possible, make a cut about one-third the diameter of the log. This allows the sawyer to step back from the log on the final cut.

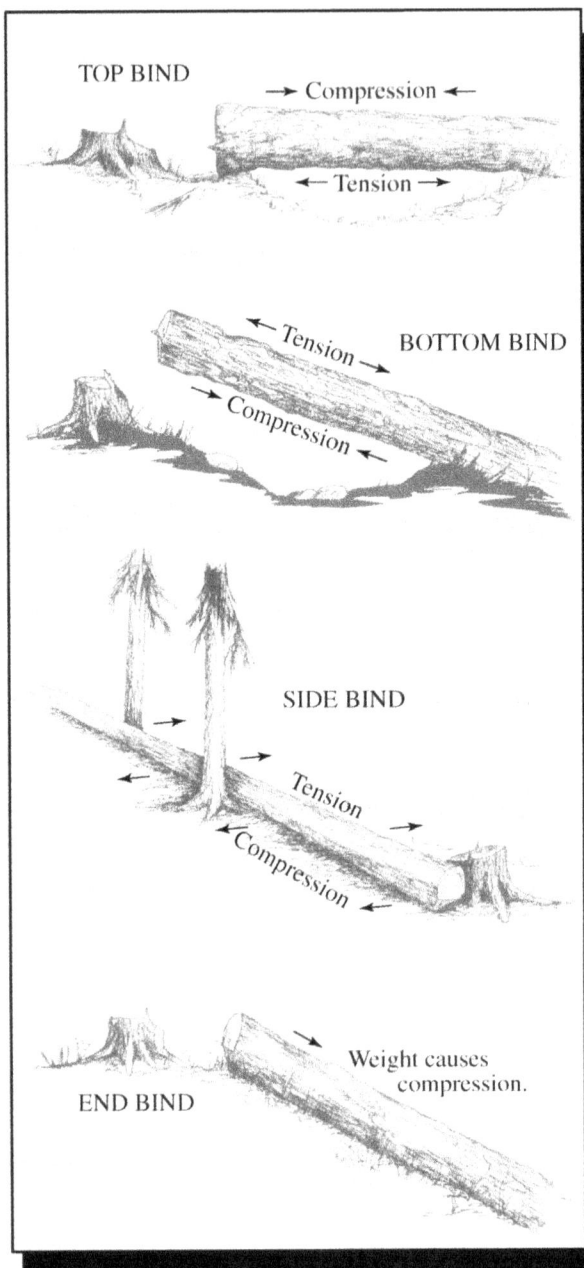

Figure 48—There are four types of binds. A log can have a combination of two or more binds.

Points to Remember When Planning the Cut

- Do a complete sizeup. Identify the hazards and establish your escape routes and safety zones.
- Use objects such as rocks, stumps (if they are tall enough), and sound standing trees (with no overhead hazards) to

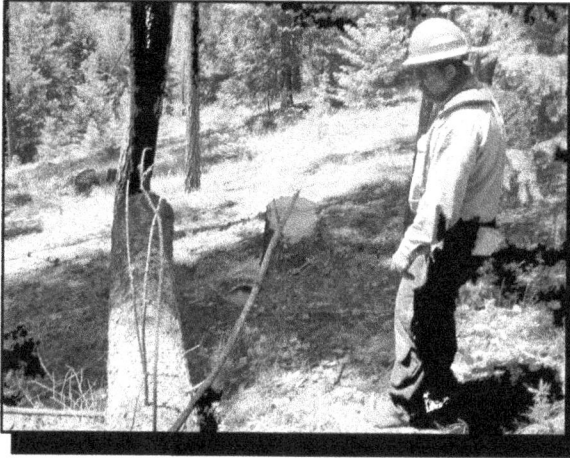

Figure 49—Determine the offside (usually the downhill side), and stay clear of that side when you are single bucking.

protect you from the log if it springs sideways toward you when you finish the cut.

- Remember that removing a single section of log may require that other binds be eliminated first.
- Make angled bucking cuts, wide on top and on the offside, so that a single section of log can be rolled away from the rest of the log.
- Buck small sections of the log that will be easy to control when they begin moving.
- Be aware that binds and potential log movement will change as you cut. Reevaluate them as necessary.
- Warn workers who are working in and below an active cutting area. Give them time to move to a safe location. Verify their safety, visually and verbally.
- Announce when a bucking operation has been completed.
- Ensure that all logs are completely severed when they are bucked.
- Use flagging to mark an incompletely bucked log as a hazard.
- Never approach a cutting operation from below.

Single-Bucking Techniques

New sawyers should master the skill of single bucking before learning double bucking. If new sawyers can handle a long two-person saw alone, they have mastered the principles of keeping the saw running smoothly without buckling. Thinner, lighter felling saws are harder to use for single bucking than the stiffer, heavier bucking saws.

The reasons to single buck include:
- The sawyer starts out double bucking and needs to finish the cut from one side because of safety considerations or log movement.
- The log is too large for the length of the saw, so one handle has to be removed to increase the effective length of the saw. The end of the saw can be drawn into the log once the handle has been taken off, allowing shavings in the gullets to be removed when the end of the saw leaves the log.
- The sawing sequence starts or ends with underbucking, which can be done only by a single sawyer.

When making compound cuts, the length of the cut determines the length of saw that is required. The saw does not work as efficiently in a sloping or compound cut as it does in a straight cut. The more angle that is placed on a compound cut, the less effectively the saw will work. Compound cuts can make sawing difficult.

Single Bucking With No Bind: Top Cutting

- Remove the bark where the cut will be made.
- Lay the unsheathed saw on its side over the log. Sprinkle lubricant on both sides of the saw.
- Hold the saw with your dominant hand and guide the back of the saw with the other hand for a few strokes until the saw is securely in the kerf.
- Insert wedges as soon as they will clear the saw, driving them snug. Do not hit the back of the saw with the wedge.
- Lubricate the blade as needed just before the push stroke. On a smaller log, the sawyer may be able to lubricate the far side of the saw just before the pull stroke. Lubricate both sides of the saw blade equally.
- As you finish the cut, use only the teeth at the end of the saw blade. This technique prevents the log from damaging the "production" cutters near the center of the saw if the log rolls or pinches the saw.

Single Bucking With Top Bind: Underbucking Required

Underbucking is used when the log has a top bind and you can get under the log. Sometimes, a V-notch can be chopped out of the top of the log, then finished with underbucking. More frequently, the first cut must be started from the top because the top of the log is under compression. If the compression is not corrected, the kerf may close and pinch the saw.

After you have inserted the wedges and driven them snug, continue cutting down from the top, leaving enough uncut wood to support the log's weight. Because the top of the log is under compression, the bottom is under tension. The more compression you relieve, the greater the tension on the bottom of the log. The log will start to equalize this pressure by exerting pressure on the wedges. If you use two or more wedges spaced at the 10 and 2 o'clock positions, you can spread the force over a larger area. If only one wedge is used at the 12 o'clock position, all the energy is directed to that relatively small area.

Listen for the sounds of wood fibers popping as they are severed as an indication of the intensity of compression and tension. The louder the sound, the stronger the forces at work.

Watch the kerf to detect log movement. Position yourself so you can detect a slight opening or closing of the kerf. This is the best indicator of the log's reaction on the release cut. If the bind cannot be evaluated, proceed with caution. It may be necessary to move the saw back and forth slowly to prevent the saw from getting bound as compression pressure closes the kerf. Cut just far enough to place a wedge. Continue cutting. Watch the kerf. If the kerf starts to open, the log has a bottom bind. If the kerf starts to close, the log has a top bind.

Remove the saw from the top cut and prepare to finish the cut from the bottom by underbucking. A log or rock can be placed under one side of the cut, supporting the log so it will be less likely to drop as far as the ground when the cut is completed.

Underbucking—During sizeup, you determined which side of the severed log probably would remain the most stationary, providing the anchor point for the underbuck. A common mistake is to place the underbuck on the side that is easiest to reach. If this side of the log moves, the saw or ax handle could be damaged.

To underbuck, use a mechanical underbuck or plant an ax in the log (after removing the bark) so the handle can be used as a support for the back of the saw (figure 50). Line up the underbuck grooves in the ax handle with the top saw kerf and forcefully swing the ax into the log.

Figure 50—An ax planted in the lower part of the log can work as an underbuck.

Place the back of the inverted saw in the underbuck groove. The saw typically starts at an angle of about 45 degrees from horizontal. Your guiding hand holds the back of the saw. With a light downward pressure on the underbuck, push the saw forward. Pressure on the underbuck needs to be consistent on the push and pull strokes.

Oil in the underbuck groove will help the saw run easily and will reduce wear on the ax handle. Adjust the handle angle to allow room for the saw to be inserted and for the underbuck to be parallel to the saw kerf, but offset slightly closer to the ax head unless you are underbucking a compound cut.

If I'm finishing a cut by underbucking, I make sure that my undercut does **not** exactly meet the top cut. Rather, I align the saw on the ax handle so the saw is offset about a half an inch from the top cut in the direction of the ax head. When the log breaks away and drops, the saw is protected by remaining in the kerf. If the technique is reversed, the moving log will drive the saw into the ax, possibly damaging the ax and injuring the sawyer.

If you are underbucking a compound cut, the cuts must match exactly. Any offset could prevent the log from being freed. If the cuts do not match, several more wedges may have to be placed in the top cut to provide additional bearing pressure on the kerf faces, holding the log in place. If there is a chance that the wedges will not hold, remove the saw and start another cut, rather than risk damaging the saw.

After several strokes, you can remove your hand and continue normal cutting. With continued downward pressure, the end of the saw will be doing more of the cutting and the saw blade will level out. As the cut nears completion, be prepared in case the severed log drops.

Often the wedges hold the log stationary after the cut is completed. To remove the hanging wedges, stand on the near side and reach across the top of the log to remove the offside hanging wedge. Then remove the near-side wedge.

Single Bucking With Top Bind: Top Cutting

Several methods can be used to buck a log with top bind that does not have enough room underneath for underbucking.

All sawing will be from the top. After removing the bark and beginning the cut, wedge the log well to keep the kerf open. Follow the instructions for wedging given earlier. Periodically, drive all the wedges until they are snug. Do not allow the wedges to contact the saw.

The cut will want to open up at the bottom. Place a log or other material under the log segment that will drop when the cut has been completed, reducing the distance the severed section of log will fall and helping to direct it to the place you want it to go.

The severed log may roll. A log that drops and rolls may damage the saw. Inserting metal hanging wedges at the 10 o'clock and 2 o'clock positions across the kerf will reduce the likelihood that the log will roll.

For very heavy logs with serious binds, a steel plate can be driven into the saw kerf as added insurance that the kerf will not close. Because steel plates are thin, they can be driven deeply without spreading the log apart. Steel plates are easier to drive than wedges and provide a large surface area to hold back the top bind. I rig these plates with a lanyard that can be secured to an ax placed on top of the log. This technique prevents the plate from dropping onto the saw when the log is released. Often there is enough bind on the steel plate to keep it in place. I also use lanyards on my pair of hanging wedges to prevent them from dropping onto the saw.

Single Bucking With Bottom Bind: Top Cutting

When there is bottom bind and too little room to get the saw underneath for an undercut, all the cutting will be done from the top. The main problem with bottom binds is that standard wedging does not help. In addition, when the log is severed, sections of the log may drop or roll, possibly damaging the saw blade.

Cut the log as explained for top cutting with single bucking. Place a small plastic wedge snugly at the top of the cut. Do not drive the wedge in.

When this wedge starts to drop into the kerf and the kerf is beginning to open, drive two fan-shaped metal hanging wedges across the kerf at the 10 and 2 o'clock positions to slow the opening of the kerf and keep the log from settling or rolling.

As the kerf opens at the top, the uncut wood is under more and more compression. If the force becomes too great, the uncut wood may slab off, possibly damaging the saw. To prevent slabbing, the sawyer needs to keep sawing or even speed up sawing to keep the kerf opening and relieve the compression pressure. When the log is sawed through, the log's weight may pull out the metal wedges, allowing the log to drop and roll.

Perhaps the best technique to reduce the effects of a bottom bind is to insert a stick into the opening saw kerf just before driving the hanging wedges. A straight, finger-sized limb about a foot long can be inserted (figure 51) into the opening kerf at the top of the log (do not use plastic wedges).

As the kerf continues to open, the stick slides into the kerf. The stick will not drop to the back of the saw because it is too thick. As the cut is completed, the two halves of the severed log will hinge on the stick. The bottom opens up, allowing the saw to drop free.

Figure 51—A stick dropped into the kerf on a log with bottom bind will serve as a pivot when the log is cut through. This is a lost trick that is very practical and can prevent damage to the saw.—Now You're Logging, by Bus Griffiths, with permission of Harbour Publishing, Madeira Park, BC, Canada

Single Bucking With Bottom Bind: Under-bucking

If you have bottom bind and can get under the log, make the first cut from the bottom. In this case, wedging is not as critical. If the first cut is from the top, fan-shaped metal

wedges can reduce the speed with which the kerf opens. A stick can be inserted into the opening top cut if the log is large enough for the stick to fit into the kerf.

Finish the top cut, trying to match the bottom cut exactly. Offset cuts are not used unless you are finishing with an undercut.

Single Bucking With End Bind

If more than one cut is being made on a log, as is often the case during trail clearing, I usually make the first cut at the largest diameter, especially if it is uphill. This reduces the amount of end bind pressure on the second cut.

If you are cutting down directly from the top, use more plastic wedges around the cut, especially as the cut progresses below the centerline of the log. The wedges will reduce the possibility of binding.

Single Bucking With Side Bind

This is one of the most difficult and hazardous binding situations.

If there is room below the log for the end of the saw to clear, cut the side with compression wood first. The finish cut is on the side with tension wood. Alternately saw and chop out wood with an ax. The saw should be in a nearly vertical position. Always find a safe position before making the finish cut.

If the log is on the ground in a side-bind situation, options are limited. For trees larger than 20 inches in diameter, the only options are to place a cut beyond the side bind area or to cut out the area with an ax.

Double-Bucking Techniques

New sawyers should master the skills of single bucking before learning double bucking. The reasons to double buck include:
• Large logs can be sawed more easily by two sawyers.
• Two sawyers can transport equipment more easily than one.
  Attach both saw handles before removing the sheath.

When this wedge starts to drop into the kerf and the kerf is beginning to open, drive two fan-shaped metal hanging wedges across the kerf at the 10 and 2 o'clock positions to slow the opening of the kerf and keep the log from settling or rolling.

As the kerf opens at the top, the uncut wood is under more and more compression. If the force becomes too great, the uncut wood may slab off, possibly damaging the saw. To prevent slabbing, the sawyer needs to keep sawing or even speed up sawing to keep the kerf opening and relieve the compression pressure. When the log is sawed through, the log's weight may pull out the metal wedges, allowing the log to drop and roll.

Perhaps the best technique to reduce the effects of a bottom bind is to insert a stick into the opening saw kerf just before driving the hanging wedges. A straight, finger-sized limb about a foot long can be inserted (figure 51) into the opening kerf at the top of the log (do not use plastic wedges).

As the kerf continues to open, the stick slides into the kerf. The stick will not drop to the back of the saw because it is too thick. As the cut is completed, the two halves of the severed log will hinge on the stick. The bottom opens up, allowing the saw to drop free.

Figure 51—A stick dropped into the kerf on a log with bottom bind will serve as a pivot when the log is cut through. This is a lost trick that is very practical and can prevent damage to the saw.—*Now You're Logging, by Bus Griffiths, with permission of Harbour Publishing, Madeira Park, BC, Canada*

Single Bucking With Bottom Bind: Under-bucking

If you have bottom bind and can get under the log, make the first cut from the bottom. In this case, wedging is not as critical. If the first cut is from the top, fan-shaped metal wedges can reduce the speed with which the kerf opens. A stick can be inserted into the opening top cut if the log is large enough for the stick to fit into the kerf.

Finish the top cut, trying to match the bottom cut exactly. Offset cuts are not used unless you are finishing with an undercut.

Single Bucking With End Bind

If more than one cut is being made on a log, as is often the case during trail clearing, I usually make the first cut at the largest diameter, especially if it is uphill. This reduces the amount of end bind pressure on the second cut.

If you are cutting down directly from the top, use more plastic wedges around the cut, especially as the cut progresses below the centerline of the log. The wedges will reduce the possibility of binding.

Single Bucking With Side Bind

This is one of the most difficult and hazardous binding situations.

If there is room below the log for the end of the saw to clear, cut the side with compression wood first. The finish cut is on the side with tension wood. Alternately saw and chop out wood with an ax. The saw should be in a nearly vertical position. Always find a safe position before making the finish cut.

If the log is on the ground in a side-bind situation, options are limited. For trees larger than 20 inches in diameter, the only options are to place a cut beyond the side bind area or to cut out the area with an ax.

Double-Bucking Techniques

New sawyers should master the skills of single bucking before learning double bucking. The reasons to double buck include:

- Large logs can be sawed more easily by two sawyers.
- Two sawyers can transport equipment more easily than one.
  Attach both saw handles before removing the sheath.

Do not use a saw with damaged handles or handles that are difficult to remove. After the sheath has been removed, the uphill sawyer normally hands the saw to the downhill sawyer by grasping one handle and the middle of the saw blade with the teeth facing away from the downhill sawyer who is receiving the saw.

Usually the uphill sawyer (the primary sawyer, who will finish the cut) lubricates the saw and positions a guiding hand on the back of the saw for the first few strokes.

If you are planning to roll the log out of the way, be sure to make a compound cut. The goal is for the sections of log to have as little surface resistance against each other as possible. The larger the log, the more careful the planning needs to be for the compound cut. Make the cuts where you will be safe and you will be able to move the log.

Your dominant hand (the power hand) should be placed firmly around the saw's handle. Your other hand can rest on top of the handle to guide the saw and to help you maintain your balance. Your dominant hand pulls the saw straight back to the side of your body. Sawyers often grip the non-power handle too tightly. This tends to pull the saw across their body.

Always pull. Never push! Allow your partner to pull. Pushing may cause the saw to buckle.

As one sawyer pulls, the other sawyer keeps a relaxed grip on the handle. The sawyer neither pushes nor holds back. Holding back is called riding the saw, which makes it harder for the other sawyer to pull. Your partner will not like this.

If you momentarily relax your grip, the saw will reposition itself in your hand for the pull stroke. Relaxing your grip also increases circulation in your hands and reduces fatigue.

If one sawyer needs to change body position (to drop to a kneeling position, for instance), the other sawyer needs to adjust the angle of the saw to accommodate the change.

Wedges should be placed as soon as there is room to insert them behind the back of the saw. Usually for large logs, two wedges are inserted at the 10 and 2 o'clock positions and driven firmly until they are snug. If the wedges are not snug, the saw could be damaged.

Be sure the saw travels into and out of the kerf in a straight line. Look down the saw toward the other sawyer to make sure the saw is traveling in a straight line.

If the log is going to be finished up by single bucking, whenever *either* sawyer determines it is time to stop sawing, both sawyers stop. If you are on the downhill side, you should quit sawing and leave whenever you feel you are in jeopardy. Do not allow your judgment to be swayed by your partner. Each partner must honor the other's request without pressure.

On flat terrain, be sure that the arc of the saw remains parallel to the ground. Do not raise one end of the saw higher than the other.

Usually the bottom bark has not been removed. Carefully look at the shavings. When they change to the color of the bark, the log has been severed and only the bark is holding it. If the log falls on mineral soil, the impact can force rocks into the bark. The rocks can dull the saw's teeth. Usually the cut is stopped when wood-colored fibers are no longer being removed.

When the cut is finished, or when it is being finished by single bucking, remove the handle on the downhill side of the saw and allow the uphill sawyer to pull the saw free. Make sure the downhill sawyer is in a safe location before the uphill sawyer continues the cut.

Do not remove the wedges before removing the saw. The wedges may be holding the log in position. If they are removed first, the severed log may shift, binding the saw. If the wedges are loose enough to be lifted straight up, it is safe to do so—but do not wiggle them out. Once the saw is free, the wedges can be removed safely from the uphill side. Be prepared for the log to move.

Crosscut saw cuts need to be made where the cuts are safe and in a manner that allows the log to be removed. Sawyers may need to make additional cuts to meet the visual or trail clearing width objectives once the log has been removed.

Do not use a saw with damaged handles or handles that are difficult to remove. After the sheath has been removed, the uphill sawyer normally hands the saw to the downhill sawyer by grasping one handle and the middle of the saw blade with the teeth facing away from the downhill sawyer who is receiving the saw.

Usually the uphill sawyer (the primary sawyer, who will finish the cut) lubricates the saw and positions a guiding hand on the back of the saw for the first few strokes.

If you are planning to roll the log out of the way, be sure to make a compound cut. The goal is for the sections of log to have as little surface resistance against each other as possible. The larger the log, the more careful the planning needs to be for the compound cut. Make the cuts where you will be safe and you will be able to move the log.

Your dominant hand (the power hand) should be placed firmly around the saw's handle. Your other hand can rest on top of the handle to guide the saw and to help you maintain your balance. Your dominant hand pulls the saw straight back to the side of your body. Sawyers often grip the non-power handle too tightly. This tends to pull the saw across their body.

Always pull. Never push! Allow your partner to pull. Pushing may cause the saw to buckle.

As one sawyer pulls, the other sawyer keeps a relaxed grip on the handle. The sawyer neither pushes nor holds back. Holding back is called riding the saw, which makes it harder for the other sawyer to pull. Your partner will not like this.

If you momentarily relax your grip, the saw will reposition itself in your hand for the pull stroke. Relaxing your grip also increases circulation in your hands and reduces fatigue.

If one sawyer needs to change body position (to drop to a kneeling position, for instance), the other sawyer needs to adjust the angle of the saw to accommodate the change.

Wedges should be placed as soon as there is room to insert them behind the back of the saw. Usually for large logs, two wedges are inserted at the 10 and 2 o'clock positions and driven firmly until they are snug. If the wedges are not snug, the saw could be damaged.

Be sure the saw travels into and out of the kerf in a straight line. Look down the saw toward the other sawyer to make sure the saw is traveling in a straight line.

If the log is going to be finished up by single bucking, whenever *either* sawyer determines it is time to stop sawing, both sawyers stop. If you are on the downhill side, you should quit sawing and leave whenever you feel you are in jeopardy. Do not allow your judgment to be swayed by your partner. Each partner must honor the other's request without pressure.

On flat terrain, be sure that the arc of the saw remains parallel to the ground. Do not raise one end of the saw higher than the other.

Usually the bottom bark has not been removed. Carefully look at the shavings. When they change to the color of the bark, the log has been severed and only the bark is holding it. If the log falls on mineral soil, the impact can force rocks into the bark. The rocks can dull the saw's teeth. Usually the cut is stopped when wood-colored fibers are no longer being removed.

When the cut is finished, or when it is being finished by single bucking, remove the handle on the downhill side of the saw and allow the uphill sawyer to pull the saw free. Make sure the downhill sawyer is in a safe location before the uphill sawyer continues the cut.

Do not remove the wedges before removing the saw. The wedges may be holding the log in position. If they are removed first, the severed log may shift, binding the saw. If the wedges are loose enough to be lifted straight up, it is safe to do so—but do not wiggle them out. Once the saw is free, the wedges can be removed safely from the uphill side. Be prepared for the log to move.

Crosscut saw cuts need to be made where the cuts are safe and in a manner that allows the log to be removed. Sawyers may need to make additional cuts to meet the visual or trail clearing width objectives once the log has been removed.

Felling

Except for firefighting and wilderness trail work, it is not common to fell trees with a crosscut saw. Much of my experience in felling with a crosscut saw was to obtain native building material for bridges, cribbing, puncheon, shake bolts, replacement logs for historical structures, or green logs for construction.

Felling is a dangerous operation. The USDA Forest Service requires that crosscut saw users working for or on behalf of the agency receive the required training and are certified to perform the specific crosscut saw work they plan to do. Simply reading this book is not enough training.

Safety Considerations

Safety considerations for felling apply whether you are using chain saws or crosscut saws. The forces acting on a tree are the same, whether hand or power tools are used. But different tools require different techniques. This guide discusses the correct procedures for felling with a crosscut saw.

Larger trees often require a two-person saw, so two fallers may be in the danger zone. There are some advantages to having two fallers. An additional set of eyes and ears will be alert to danger. Crosscut saw operations are relatively quiet, so a faller often can hear the stresses of wood as pressure is being released and the noises of branches breaking above the fallers.

The most important advantage of having a second faller is a change in mental and behavioral attitude evident in good teamwork. The saying, "Two heads are better than one," applies here.

Each faller requires an escape route and an alternate route. The two fallers should not use the same escape route. If fallers need to rest during the cut, they should move to the safety zone. The rest should be as brief as possible. Sawing the back cut should progress deliberately and continuously until the tree begins to fall. Avoid rest breaks during back cutting. Additional safety considerations include:

• Remove loop- or pin-style handles to make sure they

For felling operations, if two sawyers are needed or if an observer/spotter is needed, document justification for additional personnel and the implementation process in the job hazard analysis.

don't stick before performing felling cuts. These handles on a two-person saw must detach quickly.

• Be sure all ax and saw handles are tight and in good repair.
• If metal wedges will be used, file off all "mushrooming" (deformed metal on the edges of the head) to prevent the wedge from splitting when struck.
• When sizing up the tree, determine the side of the tree where the head faller will stand. This is usually the side that best enables the faller to remove the saw from the cut and place it on the ground just before the tree falls.
• If one handle of a two-person saw is hard to remove, ensure that the handle is in the hands of the head faller who will not have to remove it.
• Drive wedges into the woody part of the tree, not the bark. Remove bark as necessary with an ax before sawing.
• Shout a warning before starting the back cut and again before finishing it.
• If several trees are being felled on steep ground, work from the bottom of the slope toward the top to avoid working around trees that have been felled.
• Do not undertake felling without all the required personal protective equipment, an ax, a set of wedges, and lubricant.

Direction of Fall

Snags and other hazard trees may be too dangerous to cut. Wedging snags produces vibrations that could dislodge material above the faller. Remember, a hazardous tree never needs to be cut. Explosives or other means can be used to bring it down with less risk.

In trail work, the purpose of felling is often to obtain construction material. You need to visualize the tree on the ground to make sure you can remove the logs you need for the project. Can a team of horses get to the site? Can the logs be winched out? Also, consider the visual effect of tree removal. Will the stump or slash be visible from the trail or structure? Is this acceptable?

Trees felled across the slope will be less likely to break, all other factors being equal. Trees felled downhill are in the air longer and pick up more speed. Uphill felling should be avoided, especially on steep slopes. The tree strikes the ground quickly, often bounces and kicks back over the stump. This is dangerous.

If a tree is not leaning more than 5 degrees from vertical and other factors are favorable (limb weight and distribution are even, winds are light, and so forth) a faller can generally drop the tree in any desired direction with proper placement of undercuts and wedges. Big trees with uneven limb distribution or noticeable lean can seldom be felled against the natural lean, even with wedges.

Situational Awareness

Analyze the tree you plan to fell:
- Health of tree (live or dead)
- Footing
- Species
- Heavy snow loading
- Size and length
- Bark soundness
- Soundness or defects
- Direction of lean
- Twin tops
- Degree of lean (slight or great)
- Type of lean (both the predominant, or head, and side lean)
- Heavy branches or uneven weight distribution
- Nesting or feeding holes
- Punky wood (swollen or sunken areas)
- Spike tops

- Knots
- Splits and frost cracks
- Rusty (discolored) knots
- Deformities, such as mistletoe damage
- Frozen wood
- Damage by lightning or fire

Analyze the base of the tree for:
- Thudding (hollow) sound when struck
- Insect activity
- Conks and mushrooms
- Feeding holes
- Rot and cankers
- Bark soundness
- Shelf or bracket fungi
- Resin flow
- Wounds or scars
- Unstable root system or root protrusions
- Split trunk

Examine surrounding terrain for:
- Steepness
- Stumps
- Depressions or humps in the ground
- Loose logs
- Debris that can fly back or kick up at the sawyers
- Rocks

Examine the immediate work area for:
- Snags
- People, roads, or vehicles
- Reserve (leave) trees that should not be damaged
- Powerlines
- Structures
- Widow makers
- Openings to fall trees
- Hangups
- Other trees that may be affected
- Fire-weakened trees
- Other trees that may have to be felled first
- Hazards such as trees, rocks, brush, or low-hanging limbs

Felling Sizeup

Most accidents are caused by falling debris. When you approach the tree to be felled, observe the top. Check for all overhead hazards that may come down during felling. Throughout the cut, glance regularly at the saw, the kerf, and the top of the tree.

Look at the limbs. Are they heavy enough on one side to affect the desired felling direction? Do the limbs have heavy accumulations of ice and snow?

Are the limbs entangled with the limbs of other trees? If so, they can snap off or prevent the tree from falling after it has been cut.

Is the wind strong enough to affect the tree's fall? Wind speeds higher than 15 miles per hour may be strong enough to affect the tree's fall. If so, stop felling. Strong winds may blow over other trees and snags in the area. Erratic winds require special safety considerations.

Check all snags in the immediate area for soundness. A snag may fall at any time with a gust of wind, the vibration of a tree fall, or as the snag's roots succumb to rot. If it is safe to do so, fell any snag that is a hazard in the cutting area before cutting the tree you intend to fell.

Clear small trees, brush, and debris from the base of the tree. Remove all material that could cause you to trip or lose balance. Also remove material that will interfere with your use of the saw, wedges, and ax. Don't fatigue yourself with unnecessary swamping. Remove only as much material as needed to work safely around the base of the tree and to provide escape routes.

The importance of sound holding (hinge) wood cannot be overemphasized. Determine the condition of the holding wood by sounding it with an ax. Look up while doing so, in case debris is dislodged. Check for frost cracks or other weak areas in the holding wood. The desired felling direction can be adjusted to compensate for weak areas in the holding wood. The depth of the undercut also can be adjusted to best take advantage of sound wood that can serve as holding wood.

Most trees have two natural leans: the predominant head lean and the secondary side lean. The leaning weight of the tree will be a combination of these two leans. Both leans must be considered when determining the desired felling direction. The desired felling direction can usually be chosen within 45 degrees of the combined lean, provided there is enough sound holding wood to work with, especially in the corners of the undercut.

Use a plumb bob or ax to evaluate the tree's lean. Project a vertical line up from the center of the tree's butt and determine if the tree's top lies to the right or left of the projected line.

A pistol-grip tree (one with a trunk that may be nearly horizontal near the ground before turning straight up) may appear to be leaning in one direction while most of the weight is actually leaning in another direction.

Look at the treetop from at least two different spots at right angles to each other. Do so again later during the sizeup, taking every opportunity to determine the correct lean.

In summary, during felling sizeup:
- Check for snags.
- Observe the top.
- Assess the soundness of the holding wood.
- Swamp out the base.
- Assess the lean.

Establishing Escape Routes

Look for a large, solid tree or rock for protection. The tree or rock must be at least 20 feet away from the stump and not directly behind it. Clear any debris that could trip you from the escape route. Practice your escape (figure 52).

Walk out the intended lay of the tree. Look for any

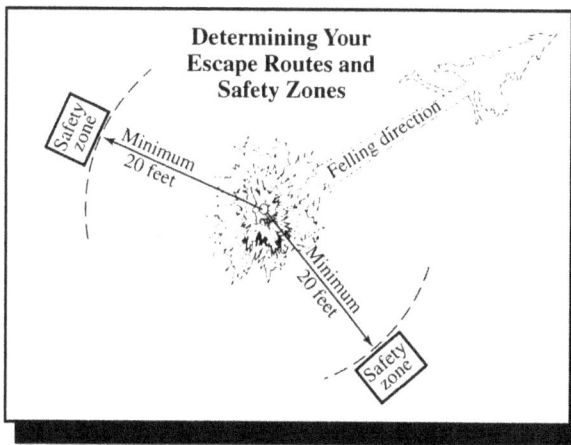

Figure 52—Keep the felling direction in mind when planning escape routes.

obstacles that could cause the tree to kick back over the stump or cause the butt to jump or pivot as the tree hits the ground. Look for any small trees or snags that could be thrown into your escape route. Ensure that the cutting area is clear of people.

Using the observations you made when walking out the intended lay of the tree, reexamine the escape route. Be sure that your chosen route (figure 53) will be the safest escape by walking out the entire length of the route—before you begin to cut.

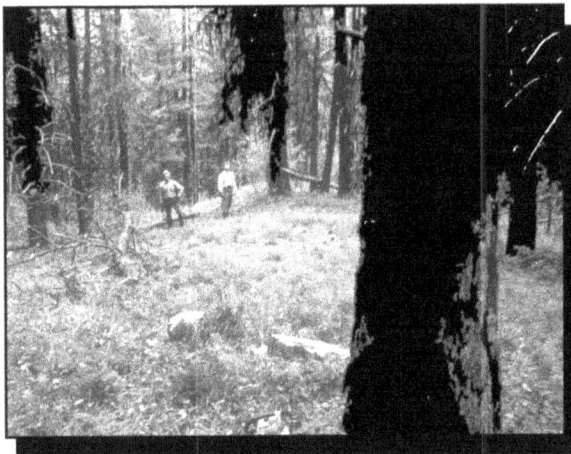

Figure 53—Check the intended lay of the tree for unwanted obstacles.

Placing the Undercut

I am going to discuss just the conventional undercut because of its broad application for all timber types and because it provides a solid foundation from which to learn additional cutting techniques.

Before beginning the undercut, prepare the tree for cutting (figure 54). Thick bark should be removed to:
- Prevent the bark from dulling the saw
- Prevent bark chunks from choking up the saw
- Make wedges more effective
- Better view the cuts to make sure they line up

I like removing the bark at the corners of the undercut because I can see the amount of holding wood that remains. Trees that have burned or that have large plates of bark or

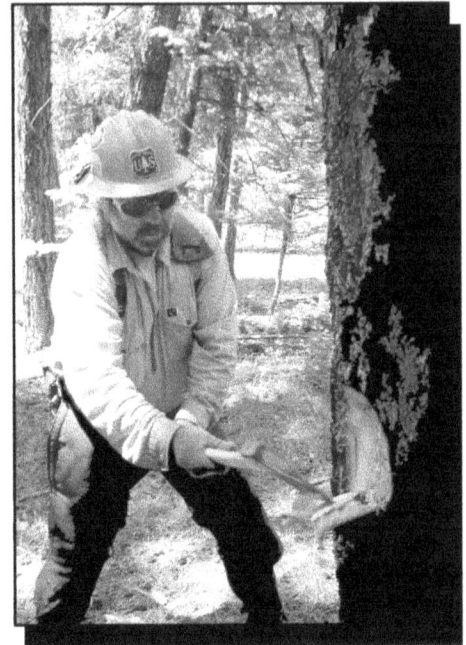

Figure 54—An ax can be used to remove bark from a log.

stringy bark often collect blowing dirt and sand that could dull the saw. In addition, removing bark may allow the saw to start into the cut more easily.

Not all trees need to have the bark removed. If the tree is small or if it has smooth, clean bark, usually there is no need to remove the bark.

It takes three cuts to fell a tree. Two cuts form the undercut (or face cut) and the third forms the back cut. The correct relationship of these cuts results in safe and effective tree felling. Before discussing the felling procedure, I will analyze the mechanics of the felling cuts. The undercut and back cut form the hinge that controls the direction and fall of the tree.

The undercut serves three purposes.
- It allows the tree to fall in a given direction by removing the tree's support in the direction of the face.
- It enables control because the tree slips off, rather than jumps off, the stump.
- It prevents the log from kicking back as it begins to fall.
  The undercut can be made by:

- Chopping out the entire undercut with an ax
- Making the undercut with a crosscut saw
- Making a horizontal cut with a crosscut saw and chopping the face out with an ax

Chopping Out the Undercut With an Ax

Although this approach may appear to be the hardest, it has advantages in certain situations. If this method is used, the cut must be level so that the back cut, which is parallel to the undercut, also will be level.

Some advantages of chopping out the undercut include:
- Chopping out the undercut is about as fast as sawing, at least on smaller trees.
- Chopping out the undercut may be best in restricted areas where one side of the tree does not offer standing room for the second sawyer or does not have adequate clearance for the end of the saw.
- Chopping out the undercut will allow the sawyer to limit the number of cuts. It is hard to apply lubricant to the bottom edge of a saw in the horizontal felling position. Chopping is especially useful if the tree is extremely pitchy.
- Chopping out the undercut is a good alternative when the saw handles cannot be vertical, when a stiff bucking saw is used, or when any combination of factors leads to an uncomfortable sawing position.
- The lower side of the tree has compression wood, which is hard on the saw set and makes work tiresome and slower.

Someone inexperienced at chopping may have trouble getting the chips to fall out properly. The best way to effectively remove the chips is to plant part, but not all, of the edge of the ax. Chop the near side of the tree, leaving the inside corner of the ax outside the tree. On the next stroke, chop the far side of the tree, leaving the outside edge of the ax outside the tree. Finish off with a keenly placed cut in the middle between the first and second cuts. A large chip will be removed (figure 55).

Using a Crosscut Saw and an Ax

Making the horizontal cut with a saw and chopping out the undercut with an ax uses both tools to their best advantage. It is often the preferred method. The horizontal saw cut is put

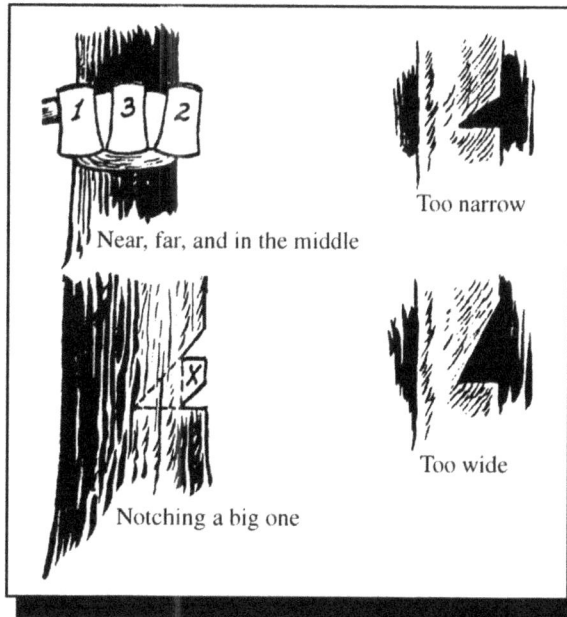

Figure 55—Notching a tree to determine the direction of fall.—Bernard Mason's *Woodsmanship* with drawings by Frederic H. Kock

in first, allowing the sawyer to place a level cut. The ax is often the best tool for the sloping cut, ensuring that it matches up with the horizontal cut and does not extend past the horizontal cut, forming a dutchman.

Making the Undercut With a Saw

This method reduces the vibration delivered to a tree, but is generally not recommended because:
- A high degree of skill is required to have both cuts meet exactly. When the cuts don't meet exactly, they create a dutchman. Careful ax work *MUST* be used to clean out the dutchman.
- Saws do not function well when they are used to cut diagonally. The body position of the faller's arms and the handle placement make for cumbersome sawing because the saw blade and handles are on a 45-degree angle. Awkward positioning also can be a safety concern.

Observe overhead hazards and look up frequently during the undercut (figure 56).

The face of the undercut should be in the general direction of the tree's lean. Depending on structures, roads, other trees, trails, and plans for removing the log, the desired felling

Figure 56—Hazard trees need to be removed to prevent anyone from working under them.

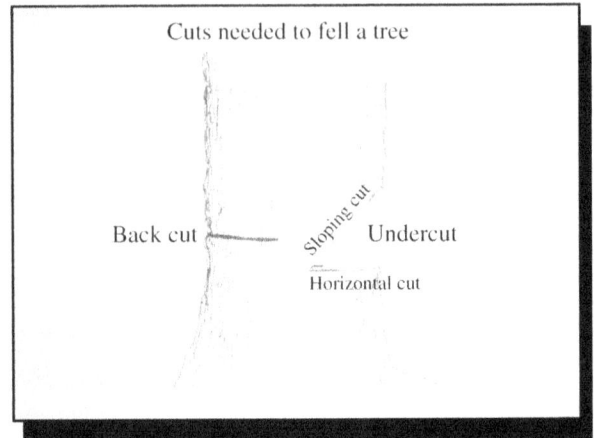

Figure 57—An undercut and a back cut are required to fell a tree. A horizontal cut and a sloping cut make up the undercut. The sloping cut is often made with an ax instead of a crosscut saw. The back cut is the third cut needed to fell a tree.

direction may be to one side or the other of the lean. Normally, the desired direction is less than 45 degrees from the lean.

I recommend that inexperienced fallers make the sloping face cut first. Remember that the saw must still be level, even though it's tilted at a 45 degree angle. It is easier to line the horizontal second cut up with the ends of the sloping cut than it would be to line a sloping cut up with the ends of the horizontal cut.

A general rule for the sloping cut is to make a 45-degree angle cut to a depth of at least one-third the diameter of the tree. The face of the cut must not close until the tree is fully committed to your planned direction of fall (figure 57). As the face closes, the holding wood breaks. If the holding wood breaks and the tree is still standing upright, the tree could fall away from the desired direction.

The horizontal cut is a level cut. If the proper relationship of the three cuts is maintained, the horizontal cut dictates the direction of fall. When there is any danger from above, the cutting should be done while the sawyer is standing, allowing the sawyer to watch the top and escape more quickly.

After selecting the desired felling direction, estimate one-third the tree's diameter and begin the horizontal cut. On larger trees you may need to place a wedge in the horizontal cut to prevent the saw from binding.

Short snags sometimes require an undercut deeper than one-third the tree's diameter to offset the tree's balance. Trees with heavy leans may not allow you to insert the horizontal cut as deep as one-third of the tree's diameter without pinching the saw.

When the horizontal cut is complete, remove the bark from an area on both sides of the kerf. The bark can be removed with an ax.

Lining up the horizontal cut with the sloping cut so that they meet, but do not cross, is one of the most difficult tasks in felling. When the cuts cross, a dutchman is formed (figure 58). If a tree with a dutchman was felled, first the dutchman would close, then the tree could split vertically (barber chair), or the holding wood could break off. Felling control would be lost. A weak tree might snap off somewhere along the bole or at the top.

It is difficult for one sawyer to make the sloping cut and the horizontal cut meet correctly on the opposite side of a large tree. This is because the sawyer cannot look behind the tree while sawing. Practicing on high stumps will help you become skilled at lining up these cuts.

The holding wood is the wood immediately behind the

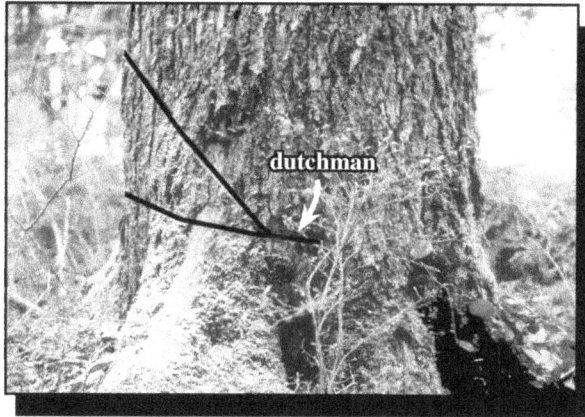

Figure 58—When the sloping cut and the horizontal cut do not meet exactly, a dutchman is formed. This kerf-wide cut makes the direction of the tree's fall harder to predict. It can also cause the tree to barber chair, lifting the log off the stump and placing the sawyers at great risk.

Figure 59—A double-bit ax is being used as a T-square to indicate the direction of fall in this 1939 photo from West Virginia. Today, hardhats and eye protection would be required dress.

undercut. The most important portion of the holding wood is in the very corners of the cut (the first 4 to 8 inches inside the bark).

If the horizontal cut is so low that cleaning it up will create too deep of an undercut, stop the horizontal cut directly above the end of the sloping cut. This will leave a step face in the undercut, but that is better than creating a dutchman or having too deep of an undercut.

The undercut needs to be cleaned out to a V-shape. Any remaining wood will cause the face to close prematurely. This causes the holding wood to break behind the closure, which can alter the direction of the fall or cause a barber chair.

The sloping face cut must be large enough to keep the tree under control until it is close to the ground. If the "mouth" is too small, the face cut will close quickly and all control of the tree will be lost. In most cases, the size of the face cut is adjusted for the lean of the tree. Never leave a dutchman in any undercut.

Once the face has been cleaned, recheck the felling direction. Place the saw back in the face and check by gunning, visualizing an imaginary line perpendicular to the saw that indicates the expected direction of fall. Alternatively, place an ax head in the face and look down the handle (figure 59). The back of the undercut should be perpendicular to the desired felling direction.

If the tree is not aimed in the direction that you want it to fall, extend the horizontal and sloping cuts as needed, keeping each cut in its original plane.

Each sawyer pulls alternately. The sawyers should be facing the direction the tree will fall. The saw is pulled back and forth with a slight upward arc at the end of the stroke.

Making the Back Cut

With a well placed undercut established, half the job is done. To successfully position the tree's direction of fall, the back cut needs to be sawn.

The relationship of this cut to the face cut is important for positioning the tree's direction of fall and the sawyer's safety. The back cut can be made from either side of the tree. Choose the safest side of the tree to cut from, (not under any lean, with a good escape route, and so forth).

The two most important elements of this cut are the holding wood and stump shot. The best way to envision these cuts is by the use of a rectangle. The bottom corner is the back of the horizontal cut. The opposite upper corner will be the back of the back cut (figure 60).

The height of the rectangle is referred to as the stump

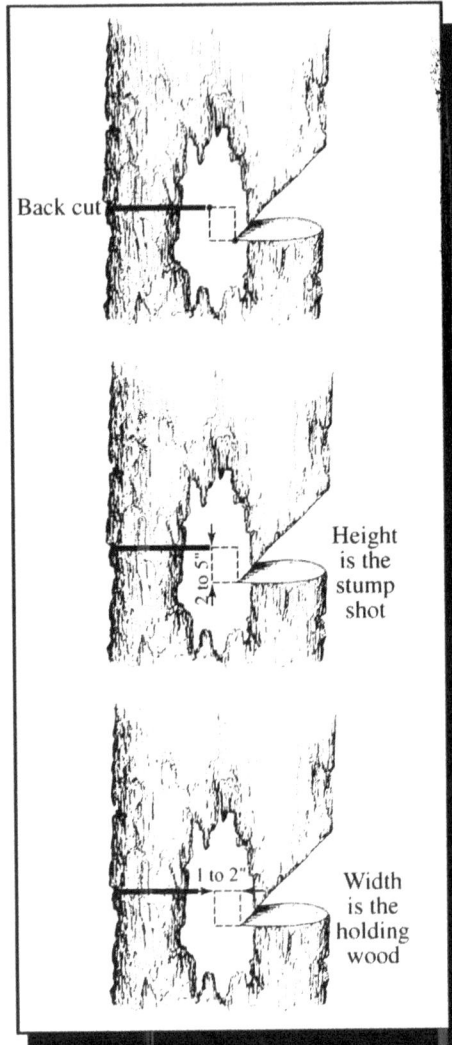

Figure 60—An imaginary rectangle can help the sawyer understand the importance of the back cut. The dimensions of this rectangle are based on a 24-inch diameter tree.

when the cut is complete. Make sure that when the back cut is finished, it will line up with the top corner of the opposite rectangle. If the cut is angled, wedging power and the height of the stump shot could be altered.

Keep at least three wedges and an ax or single jack hammer readily accessible. The ax should be within arm's reach. The size of wedges you will need depend on the tree's diameter.

If there is any wind, two wedges are recommended. The second wedge adds stability. With just one wedge in place, the tree can set up a rocking action between the holding wood and the lone wedge. A strong wind could tear out the holding wood.

Remove thick bark immediately above and below the back cut, where the wedges will be placed. The bark could compress, reducing the wedge's lifting power. Before starting the back cut, lubricate both sides of the crosscut saw. A saw in the horizontal position in the back cut is more prone to accumulate pitch than a saw used vertically for bucking. If the tree is very pitchy, the saw may need to be removed from the cut when you apply solvent. Sometimes solvent can be splashed or sprayed from the underside of the saw.

Sound a warning before the back cut is started, just in case someone has wandered into the cutting area. The sawyers position themselves with their backs toward the center of the tree. This position is natural, and also allows the sawyers to face their escape routes. The back cut should be sawn parallel to the face cut, keeping the holding wood equal from corner to corner. The sawyers need to keep an eye on the top of the tree as the back cut progresses. If the tree is a heavy leaner, each of the corners can be cut out first, finishing the cut by sawing parallel to the face cut. This technique reduces the chance that a tree might barber chair.

Once the cut provides enough clearance from the back of the saw, a wedge or wedges can be driven into place. On smaller trees, a single wedge can be used, but usually two or more wedges are needed. After every couple of inches of sawing, stop and drive the wedges in a little. Wedging redistributes the center of gravity of the standing tree by hinging the tree on the holding wood. It also prevents the tree from sitting back and binding the saw.

Observe the top of the tree to coordinate the strike of

shot. It is an antikickback device to prevent the tree from kicking back over the stump if it hits another tree on its fall. This is especially important to sawyers who are felling trees through standing timber.

The width of the rectangle is the holding wood. As the back cut is made, the sawyer must be sure not to cut this wood. Maintaining the holding wood is the key to safe and effective felling.

Hold the saw level so that the back cut will be level

each blow against the wedge with the forward sway of the tree. The wedges are easier to drive when you do so. Striking the wedge when the tree's pressure is on the wedge not only damages it, but also causes excessive vibration and could dislodge an overhead hazard.

The sawyers need to communicate so each of them knows about how many inches of holding wood remain so they can adjust their cutting to ensure that the back cut remains parallel to the face cut. A sawyer working alone needs to look around the tree periodically to accomplish this. Progressing too far and cutting the holding wood from one corner could mean the loss of felling control.

The back cut must not proceed so far toward the under-cut that it removes the holding wood. This narrow strip of holding wood must be left completely across the stump. The holding wood controls the tree's fall and prevents it from slipping off the stump prematurely.

Sound another warning when the back cut is completed and the tree is ready to fall. If the tree has not committed to fall and the holding wood is narrowing, the tree is sitting back on the wedges. Stop sawing and leave the holding wood intact. The second faller removes the saw handle and proceeds along the escape route to the safety zone. At the same time, the head faller removes the saw and places it behind the tree in a predetermined location away from the escape route. Never take the saw with you along the escape route—it could impede your progress.

With the second faller watching, the head faller drives the wedges, causing the tree to lift and commit to fall. You can see the top of the tree begin to move before you can see the saw kerf widen. The head faller proceeds along the escape route to safety before the tree actually falls.

If for any reason the sawyers feel unsafe or unsure, they should proceed immediately along the escape route. *Leave the saw wherever it lies.*

Once you've reached a safe location, both sawyers need

Fell no tree if you are uncomfortable with the task. If you have started to fell a tree but are having second thoughts, do not feel that you are committed to finishing the job in an unsafe manner. If a cut has been started but is terminated before the tree is on the ground, you MUST flag the area around the tree, declaring it a danger zone. Warn people to remain clear of the area until someone else can take the tree down.

to continue looking up for overhead hazards. There is a tendency to look at the tree as it hits the ground, leaving the sawyers unaware of limbs that may be thrown back from other trees near the stump. *LOOK UP!* If rocks or other material are dislodged when the tree hits the ground, yell a warning!

o o book can teach you all there is to know about crosscut

Concluding Principles

Nsaws and their safe use. I hope that this guide will help establish the basis for a safe learning experience. As you practice some of these techniques and come to recognize and appreciate the timeless elegance and efficiency of a finely tuned crosscut saw, bear in mind that *you* are in charge of your own well-being. With that in mind:

- Never work above your skill or certification level.

- Never be talked into something you're not comfortable doing.
- Walk away from any situation that is unsafe.
- Select the correct saw, wedges, and other accessories for the job at hand.
- Have your saws professionally sharpened—never use a misery whip!

My parting wish for you is to be

David Michael bucking a 44-inch-diameter Sitka spruce on the Tongass National Forest in Alaska (1991). Experienced sawyers will note both a dutchman and removal of holding wood in the felling cuts. These were done purposely to fell the tree in an exact spot. Such techniques should only be done by highly skilled sawyers, and then only rarely. The photo points out how much more there is to learn beyond the basics presented in this guide.

safe and content in your work using a saw that *sings!*

References Cited

Note: Visitors to the technology and development Web site (*http://www.fs.fed.us/t-d*) must provide the **username (t-d)** and **password (t-d)**.

Birkby, Robert C. 1996. Lightly on the land: the SCA manual of backcountry work skills. ISBN 1–89886–491–7. Student Conservation Association. Seattle, WA: The Mountaineers. 272 p. (Copies for sale at 603–543–1700.)

Disston, Henry, & Sons, Inc. 1902. Handbook for lumbermen. ISBN 1–879335–45–X. 162 p. (Published in 1994 by The Astragal Press, P.O. Box 239, Mendham, NJ 07945).

Griffiths, Bus. 1978. Now you're logging. ISBN 1–55017–033–3. 119 p. (Available at Harbour Publishing, P.O. Box 219, Madeira Park, BC, Canada.)

Jackson, George. 1997. Crosscut saw guards. Tech Tip 9723–2341–MTDC. Missoula, MT: U.S. Department of Agriculture, Forest Service, Missoula Technology and Development Center. 4 p. (Available at *http://www.fs.fed.us/t-d*, or call 406–329–3978.)

Mason, Bernard S., drawings by Frederic H. Kock. 1954, Woodsmanship. Library of Congress Card No. 54–5406. New York: A.S. Barnes and Co., Inc. 90 p.

Miller, Warren. 1977. (rev. 2003). Crosscut saw manual. Tech. Rep. 7771–2508–MTDC. Missoula, MT: U.S. Department of Agriculture, Forest Service, Missoula Technology and Development Center. 30 p. (Available at *http://www.fs.fed.us/t-d*, search for "crosscut," or call 406–329–3978.)

Morris, John M. 1991. Saws and Sawmills for planters and growers. ISBN 1–871315–11–5. Bedford, UK: Cranfield Press. 158 p.

Parker, George C. 1939. Organizing falling and bucking personnel. West Coast Lumberman. Jan.

Simonds Saw Co. 1919. The Simonds saws and knives catalog No. 19. 195 p. Published in 1994 by Roger K. Smith, P.O. Box 177, Athol, MA 01331. (Available at *http://www. tooltimer.com/roger*, or call 978–249–5909.)

U.S. Department of Agriculture, Forest Service. 1999. An ax to grind: parts 1 and 2 (videos). Missoula, MT: U.S. Department of Agriculture, Forest Service, Missoula Technology and Development Center. 30 minutes each. (Copies available at 406–329–3978.)

U.S. Department of Agriculture, Forest Service. 1999. Health and safety code handbook. Forest Service Handbook 6709.11. Washington, DC: U.S. Department of Agriculture, Forest Service.

U.S. Department of Agriculture, Forest Service. 1998. Handtools for trail work: parts 1 and 2 (videos). Missoula, MT: U.S. Department of Agriculture, Forest Service, Missoula Technology and Development Center. 26 minutes (part 1) and 25 minutes (part 2). (Copies available at 406–329–3978.)

Weisgerber, Bernie; Vachowski, Brian. 1999. An ax to grind: a practical ax manual. Tech. Rep. 9923–2823–MTDC. Missoula, MT: U.S. Department of Agriculture, Forest Service, Missoula Technology and Development Center. 60 p. (Available at *http://www.fs.fed.us/t-d*, search for "ax," or call 406–329–3978.)

Wolf, Jerry Taylor; Whitlock, Chuck. 2006. Chain saw and crosscut saw training course: student's guidebook. Tech Rep. 0667–2805–MTDC. Missoula, MT: U.S. Department of Agriculture, Forest Service, Missoula Technology and Development Center. 96 p. (This guidebook is included on the training course CD available at *http://www.fs.fed.us/t-d/pubs/htmlpubs/htm06672W06/* Username t-d, Password: t-d, or call 406–329–3978.)

Whitlock, Chuck; Harding, Chuck. 2000. Crosscut saw underbucking tool. Tech Tip 0223–2330–MTDC. Missoula, MT: U.S. Department of Agriculture, Forest Service, Missoula Technology and Development Center. 6 p. (Available at *http://www.fs.fed.us/t-d*, search for "crosscut," or call 406–329–3978.)

Additional References

Note: Visitors to the technology and development Web site (*http://www.fs.fed.us/t-d*) must provide the **username (t-d)** and **password (t-d)**.

Agate, Elizabeth. 1991. (rev. 1995). Toolcare: a maintenance and workshop manual. ISBN 0–946752–13–3. Wallingford, Oxfordshire, England: British Trust for Conservation Volunteers.

Anderson, Gus Y. Instructions for filing crosscut saws with the Handy Andy saw tools. Galt, ON, Canada: Shurly & Dietrich, 23 p.

Anon. 1940. Fitting redwood felling saws. Timberman. Feb.

Atkins, H. C. The development of crosscut saws and handles. The Saw Kerf. 22(7).

Bryant, Ralph Clement. 1913. Logging: the principles and general methods of operations in the United States. New York: John Wiley & Sons, Inc.

Brown, Nelson Courtland. 1934. Logging: the principles and methods of harvesting timber in the United States and Canada. John Wiley & Sons, Inc. 418 p.

Cook, D. 1981. Keeping warm with an ax: a woodcutter's manual. ISBN 0–87663–347–5. New York: Universe Books. 139 p.

Cohen, Maurice. 1981. The woodcutter's companion: a guide to locating, cutting, transporting, and storing your own firewood. ASIN 0878573281. Emmaus, PA: Rodale Press.

Conway, Steve. 1968. Timber cutting practices. ISBN 0–87930–021–3. San Francisco, CA: Miller Freeman Publications, Inc., 192 p.

Crosscut Saw Co. Catalog No. 7. 1990. Seneca Falls, NY: Crosscut Saw Co.

Crosscut Saw Co. Instructions for use and care of the crosscut saw. Seneca Falls, NY: Crosscut Saw Co. 1 p.

Curtis Saw Division Catalog. 1975. Seneca Falls, NY: Jemco Tool Corp.

Deaton, Jim. 1998. Crosscut saw reflections in the Pacific Northwest. ISBN 0–87770–675–1. YeGalleon Press. 231 p.

Dent, D. Douglas. 1974. Professional timber falling: a procedural approach. Library of Congress Catalog No. 74–29331. Portland, OR: Ryder Printing Co. 181 p.

Disston Canada Limited. 1940. Disston Catalog. Disston Canada Limited.

Disston, Henry, & Sons, Inc. 1921. Disston lumberman's handbook: a practical book of information on the construction and care of saws. Philadelphia, PA: Henry Disston & Sons, Inc.

Disston, Henry, & Sons, Inc. 1926. The saw in history. Philadelphia, PA: Henry Disston & Sons, Inc.

Disston, Henry, & Sons, Inc. 1935. Catalog No. 95. Philadelphia, PA: Henry Disston & Sons, Inc.

Drushka, Ken. 1997. Working in the woods: a history of logging on the West Coast. ISBN 1–55017–072–4. Madeira Park, BC, CN: Harbour Publishing. 304 p.

Ducommun Corp. 1930. Catalog "H." San Francisco, CA: Ducommun Corp.

Durham, Harry W. Saws: their care and treatment. New York: D. Van Nostrand Co.

E. C. Atkins and Co. 1935. Catalog No. 21. Indianapolis, IN: E.C. Atkins and Co.

Elmer, Manual Conrad. 1961. Timber. 61–13062. Boston, MA: The Christopher Publishing House.

G. Anderson Saw Gauge Manufacturing Co. 1939. Saw filing simplified: by use of the Anderson sawfiling tools for crosscut saws. Seattle, WA: G. Anderson Saw Gauge Manufacturing Co. 16 p.

General Services Administration, Federal Supply Service, Standardization Division. 1966. Saw: bow and crosscut, one-man and two-man. 1966. Interim Federal specifications GGG–S–0064a. Washington, DC: General Services Administration. July 20.

Goodman, W. L. 1964. The history of woodworking tools. ASIN 0679500316. London, England: G. Bell & Sons, Ltd. 208 p.

Gosnell, Ron. 1983. How to sharpen a crosscut saw. American Forests. Sept. 10 p.

Graham, Arthur. 1937. Filing crosscut saws. Timberman. Aug. 97 p.

Hallman, Richard. 2005. Handtools for trail work: 2005 edition. Tech. Rep. 0523–2810–MTDC. Missoula, MT: U.S. Department of Agriculture, Forest Service, Missoula Technology and Development Center. 54 p. (Available at *http://www.fs.fed.us/t-d*, search for "handtool," or call 406–329–3978.)

Hesselbarth, Woody; Vachowski, Brian; Davies, Mary Ann. 2007. Trail construction and maintenance notebook. Tech. Rep. 0723–2806–MTDC. Missoula, MT: U.S. Department of Agriculture, Forest Service, Missoula Technology and Development Center. 166 p. (Available at *http://www.fhwa.dot.gov/environment/rectrails/trailpub.htm*)

Holly, H. W. 1902. The art of saw filing. New York: John Wiley & Sons.

Kauffman, Henry J. 1972. American axes: a survey of their development and their makers. ISBN 0–8289–0138–4. Brattleboro, VT: Stephen Greene Press. 151 p.

Keller, David Neal. 1983. Cooper Industries, 1833–1983: ISBN 0–8214–0751–1. Athens, OH: Ohio University Press.

Koroleff, A. 1947. Pulpwood cutting: efficiency of technique. Montreal, Quebec, CN: Canadian Pulp and Paper Association, Woodlands Section Index No. 630 (B–7–a).

Langsner, Drew. 1978. Country woodcraft, ISBN 0–87857–200–7. Emmaus, PA: Rodale Press. 394 p.

Leete, F. A. 1920. Lumbering and wood-working industries in the U.S. and Canada.

Lind, Carol J. 1978. Big timber, big men. ISBN 0–88839–020–3. Seattle, WA: Hancock House Publishing, Inc.

Mason, Bernard S. 1945. Woodsmanship. Library of Congress No. 54–5406. New York: A.S. Barnes and Company. 90 p.

Mattson, Richard C. A course in saw filing. U.S. Department of Agriculture, Forest Service, Region 1, CCC Camp F-102. Coeur d' Alene, ID: Kaniksu National Forest, ID.

McLaren, Peter. 1929. Ax manual of Peter McLaren. Philadelphia, PA: Fayette R. Plumb, Inc. 84 p.

Mercer, Henry C. 1960. Ancient carpenters' tools. Doylestown, PA: Bucks County Historical Society.

Patterson, Lillie. 1967. Lumberjacks of the north woods. Library of Congress No. 67–14625. Champaign, IL: Garrard Publishing Co.

Richardson, M. T. 1889. Practical blacksmithing. New York: Weathervane Books.

Serry, Victor. 1963. British sawmilling practice. London, England: Ernest Benn, Ltd.

Simmons, Fred C. 1951. Northeastern logger's handbook. Agric. Handb. No. 6. Washington, DC: U.S. Department of Agriculture. 160 p.

Simonds Saws & Knives. Catalog. 1919. Simonds Manufacturing Co. Reprinted by Roger Smith Publishing, Athol, MA. March 1994. 195 p.

Simonds Crosscut Saws Handles and Tools. Catalog 77. Fitchburg, MA: Simonds Saw and Steel Co.

Simonds Saw and Steel Co. 1953. Catalog: crosscut saws, pulpwood saws. Fitchburg, MA: Simonds Saw and Steel Co.

Simonds Saw and Steel Co. 1947. How to file a crosscut saw. Fitchburg, MA: Simonds Saw and Steel Co. 25 p.

Simonds Saw and Steel Co. 1946. Catalog 46. Fitchburg, MA: Simonds Saw and Steel Co.

Singh, S. Niranjan. 1959. Maintenance of crosscut saws. Indian Forester. Sept.: 564-571.

Spear & Jackson, Ltd. 1936. Catalogue E4. Sheffield, England: Spear & Jackson, Ltd.

Stack, Emmett G. 1942. New type falling saw patented. The Timberman. March: 51.

Stovall, Charles. 1944. A manual for fallers, buckers, scalers and bull bucks. The Timberman. 30 p.

Taylor, Jay L. B. 1916. Handbook for rangers and woodsmen. New York: John Wiley & Sons, Inc.

Twitchell, Mary. 1978. Wood energy: a practical guide to heating with wood. ISBN 0–88266–145–0. Charlotte, VT: Garden Way Publishing. 172 p.

Underhill, Roy. 1983. The woodwright's companion: exploring traditional woodcraft. ISBN No. 0–8078–1540–3. Chapel Hill, NC: The University of North Carolina Press. 191 p.

United Nations Food and Agriculture Organization. 1982. Basic technology in forest operations. Tech. Pap. 36, ISBN 92–5–101260–1. Rome: United Nations Food and Agriculture Organization. 132 p.

U.S. Department of Agriculture, Forest Service, Missoula Technology and Development Center. 1974. Crosscut saws: description, sharpening, reconditioning. Tech. Rep. 7471–0006–MTDC. Missoula, MT: U.S. Department of Agriculture, Forest Service, Missoula Technology and Development Center. 139 p.

U.S. Department of Agriculture, Forest Service, Missoula Technology and Development Center. 1989. Lightweight crosscut saws. Equip Tips 8951–2312–MTDC. Missoula, MT: U.S. Department of Agriculture, Forest Service, Missoula Technology and Development Center. 1 p.

U.S. Department of Agriculture, Forest Service. 1922. Sharpening crosscut saws. Government Printing Office No. 8–5157. Washington, DC: U.S. Department of Agriculture. 22 p.

U.S. Navy, Bureau of Naval Personnel (NAVPERS). 1970. Logging operations. In: Basic construction techniques for houses and small buildings simply explained. ISBN 0-486-20242-9. New York: Dover Publications, Inc. 568 p.

Watson, Aldren A. 1979. The six-foot two-man crosscut. Blair and Ketchum's Country Journal. 7 p.

Weisgerber, Bernie. 1999. An ax to grind: a practical ax manual. Tech. Rep. 9923–2823P–MTDC. Missoula, MT: U.S. Department of Agriculture, Forest Service, Missoula Technology and Development Center. 60 p. (Available at *http://www.fs.fed.us/t-d* Username t-d, Password t-d; search for "crosscut," or call 406–329–3978.)

Wilbur, C. Keith. 1992. Home building and woodworking in colonial America. ISBN 1–56440–019–0. Old Saybrook, CT: Globe Pequot Press. 121 p.

Workers' Compensation Board of British Columbia. 1981. Fallers' and bucker's handbook: describing practical methods and procedures for falling and bucking timber safely. 7th ed. Vancouver, BC, CN: Workers' Compensation Board of British Columbia.

Sources for Crosscut Saws and Accessories

The following list of crosscut saw and accessories providers is neither intended to be all inclusive nor to imply USDA Forest Service approval or recommendation of these suppliers.

Vintage Saws

Electronic auction sites such as the *eBay* Web site (*http://www.ebay.com*), yard sales, and antique shops are likely places to buy a used crosscut saw and sharpening tools. Small businesses selling vintage crosscut saws sometimes can be located though Internet search engines. Most trail workers consider a well-tuned vintage saw to be superior to a new saw. New saws usually need sharpening before they are suitable for use.

Agency employees should search the back corners of their fire caches, guard stations, and work centers for vintage crosscut saws that can be restored and used to outfit the crew. Don't throw them out! It is not difficult to find someone to professionally restore and sharpen vintage saws at a reasonable cost.

New Crosscut Saws and Accessories

- **The Crosscut Saw Co.** sells new and vintage crosscut saws and tools.
  Crosscut Saw Co.
  P.O. Box 787
  Seneca Falls, NY 13148
  Phone: 315–568–5755
  Web site: *http://www.crosscutsaw.com*
- **Flicker Forge** offers replica vintage saw handles.
  Flicker Forge (Japheth Howard)
  39184 School House Rd.
  Salisbury, MO 65281
  Phone: 660–777–3508
  Fax: 660–777–3302
  Web site: *http://www.flickerforge.com*
- **Jim's Crosscut Saws** sells reconditioned saws and accessories, and sharpens saws.
  Jim's Crosscut Saws (Jim Talburt)
  7914 Northbank Rd.
  Roseburg, OR 97470
  Phone: 541–673–6940
  Web site: *http://www.jimscrosscutsaws.com*

- **Lehman's** offers several one- and two-person saws and handles.
  Lehman's
  P.O. Box 41
  One Lehman Circle
  Kidron, OH 44636
  Phone orders: 1–877–438–5346
  Customer service: 1–888–438–5346
  Fax: 1-888-780-4975
  Web site: *http://www.Lehmans.com*

- **Tuatahi Axes and Saws** offers crosscut saws for forest workers and for sawyers who compete in races. Bailey's is the United States distributor for Tuatahi products.
  Tuatahi Axes and Saws
  203 High St.
  Masterton
  New Zealand
  Phone: (011) 646–377–3728
  Fax: (011) 646–377–5343

- **Bailey's**
  P.O. Box 550
  44650 Highway 101
  Laytonville, CA 95454
  Phone: 707–984–6133
  Fax: 707–984–8115
  Web site: *http://www.baileys-online.com*

- **Woodcraft** offers at least two types of crosscut saws.
  Woodcraft
  P.O. Box 1686
  Parkersburg, WV 26102–1686
  Phone: 304–442–5412
  Web site: *http://www.woodcraft.com*

Subscribe to Crosscut Saw Bulletin

The *Crosscut Saw Bulletin* is an occasional electronic newsletter about crosscut saws and the people who use them. David Michael is the editor. To subscribe to this free newsletter, send an e-mail message to *demichael@fs.fed.us*. Identify yourself by name, e-mail address, and agency unit or club affiliation, if applicable.

Felling crew working on a Douglas fir in Skagit County, Washington, 1902.—*USDA Forest Service photo, photographed by D.R. Kinsey*

Single copies of this document may be ordered from:

USDA Forest Service, MTDC

5785 Hwy. 10 West

Missoula, MT 59808–9361

Phone: 406–329–3978

Fax: 406–329–3719

Email: *wo_mtdc_pubs@fs.fed.us*

For additional information about this report, MTDC.

Phone: 406–329–3900

Fax: 406–329–3719

Electronic copies of MTDC's documents are available on the Internet at:

http://www.fs.fed.us/eng/pubs

USDA Forest Service and U.S. Department of the Interior Bureau of Land Management employees can search a more complete collection of MTDC's documents, videos, and CDs on their internal computer networks at:

http://fsweb.mtdc.wo.fs.fed.us/search

www.ingramcontent.com/pod-product-compliance
Lightning Source LLC
Chambersburg PA
CBHW080621030426
42336CB00018B/3039